Responding to Attack

Firefighters and Police

Other titles in the Lucent Library of Homeland Security

Defending the Borders
Deterring and Investigating Attack
Hunting Down the Terrorists
A Vulnerable America

THE
LUCENT
LIBRARY OF
HOMELAND
SECURITY

Responding to Attack

to Attack

Firefighters and Police

James D. Torr

**LUCENT
BOOKS®**

THOMSON

GALE

San Diego • Detroit • New York • San Francisco • Cleveland • New Haven, Conn. • Waterville, Maine • London • Munich

THOMSON
———∗———™
GALE

LIBRARY OF CONGRESS CATALOGING-IN-PUBLICATION DATA

Torr, James D., 1974–
   Responding to attack : firefighters and police / by James D. Torr.
    p. cm. — (The Lucent library of homeland security)
Summary: Provides an overview of our nation's attack-preparedness efforts and
describes the different roles that first responders, as well as agencies at all levels of gov-
ernment, would play in responding to the next terrorist attack on America.
Includes bibliographical references and index.
   ISBN 1-59018-375-4 (hardback : alk. paper)
   1. Civil defense—United States—Juvenile literature. 2. War on Terrorism, 2001—
Juvenile literature. 3. Terrorism—Prevention—United States—Juvenile literature. 4.
Weapons of mass destruction—Safety measures—Juvenile literature. 5. Emergency man-
agement—United States—Juvenile literature. 6. Police-fire integration—United States—
Juvenile literature. 7. War damage, Industrial—United States—Juvenile literature. [1.
Civil defense. 2. War on Terrorism, 2001– . 3. Terrorism—Prevention. 4. Weapons of mass
destruction—Safety measures.] I. Title. II. Series.
   UA927.T67 2004
   363.35'0973—dc22
                                             2003014493

Contents

Foreword

S tunned by the terrorist attacks of September 11, 2001, millions of Americans clung to President George W. Bush's advice in a September 20 live broadcast speech to "live your lives, and hug your children." His soothing words made an indelible impression on people in need of comfort and paralyzed by fear. Recent history had seen no greater emotional flood than occurred in the days following September 11, as people were united by deep shock and grief and an instinctive need to feel safe.

Searching for safety, a panicked nation urged taking extreme and even absurd measures. Immediately after the attacks, it was suggested that all aircraft passengers be restrained for the duration of flights—better to restrict the movement of all than to risk allowing one dangerous passenger to act. After the attempted bombing of a flight from Paris to Atlanta in December 2001, one *New York Times* columnist even half-seriously suggested starting an airline called Naked Air—"where the only thing you wear is a seat belt." Although such acute fear and paranoia waned as the attacks slipped further into the past, a dulled but enduring desire to overhaul national security remained.

Creating the Department of Homeland Security was one way to allay citizens' panic and fear. Congress has allocated billions to secure the nation's infrastructure, bolster communication channels, and protect precious monuments against terrorist attack. Further funding has equipped emergency responders with state-of-the-art tools such as hazardous-material suits and networked communication systems. Improved databases and intelligence-gathering tools have extended the reach of intelligence agencies, in the effort to ferret out the terrorists hiding among us. Supporters of these programs praised the Bush administration for its attention to security lapses and agreed that in the post–September 11 world, only with tighter security could Americans go about their lives free of fear and reservation.

It did not take long, however, for the sense of national unity and purpose to splinter as people advanced countless ideas for actually achieving that security. As it became evident that ensuring safety meant curtailing Americans' freedom, the price of security became a hotly debated issue. With September 11 now years in the past, and after new wars and aggression waged in its name, it is not clear that the United States is any closer to becoming what many consider impossible: an America immune to attack. As distinguished political science professor Janice Gross Stein maintains, "Military preeminence, no matter how overwhelming, does not buy the United States security from attack, even in its heartland." Whether the invasion of sovereign nations, the deaths of thousands of civilians, and the continued endangerment of American troops have made the world any safer or the United States any less vulnerable to terror is unproved.

All Americans want to feel safe; beyond that basic agreement, however, commonality ends. Thus, how to ensure homeland security, and a myriad of related questions, is one of the most compelling and controversial issues in recent history. The books in this series explore this new chapter in history and examine its successes and challenges. Annotated bibliographies provide readers with ideas for further research, while fully documented primary and secondary source quotations enhance the text. Each book in the series carefully considers a different aspect of homeland security; together they provide students with a wealth of information as well as launching points for further study and discussion.

America the Vigilant

The United States has won significant victories in its ongoing war against terrorism: the ousting of the Taliban government in Afghanistan, the arrest of dozens of al-Qaeda members and hundreds of other terrorists, and the removal of dictator Saddam Hussein from power in Iraq. Nevertheless U.S. leaders, from President George W. Bush on down, have warned Americans against being complacent or overconfident about the war against terrorism. "America is no longer protected by vast oceans," Bush said in his 2002 State of the Union address. "We are protected from attack only by vigorous action abroad, and increased vigilance at home."[1]

Other federal officials have bluntly stated that Americans should expect another terrorist attack on U.S. soil. "There will be another terrorist attack. We will not be able to stop it. . . . It's something we all have to live with,"[2] warned FBI director Robert Mueller in May 2002. In that same month Vice President Dick Cheney stated on NBC's *Meet the Press* that: "The prospects of future attack against the United States are almost certain."[3] This grim outlook is not confined to Washington, D.C.: "I don't particularly like the comments I hear of people around here saying, 'it can't happen here,'" says Des Moines, Iowa, fire chief, Ron Wakeham. "Let me tell you, being in emergency services for 30 years, it can happen here. I expect to see . . . suicide bombings here. I have no doubt that we'll see more attacks."[4]

In the face of these warnings people want to know: Is the United States prepared to respond to another terrorist attack? The answer to this question is not a simple yes or no. Dealing with another terrorist attack as destructive as—or even more destructive than—the attacks of September 11, 2001, is simply a frightening prospect. It is not surprising, therefore, that America's attack preparedness is a very sensitive and controversial issue.

On the bright side, America's overall response to September 11 is, in general, cause for confidence. While the attacks themselves were horrific, emergency workers in New York City and Washington, D.C., responded quickly and effectively to minimize damage and save lives. Beyond the incidents of individual heroism, September 11 showed that these cities' emergency-response plans, for the most part, worked.

Firefighters pull an injured man from the World Trade Center in the aftermath of the September 11 terrorist attacks. Many experts worry that America is vulnerable to another such terrorist attack.

New York City was able to coordinate hundreds of emergency workers, even though the city's Emergency Operations Center, located in one of the smaller buildings in the World Trade Center complex, was destroyed in the attacks. So many volunteers showed up to help at what became known as "Ground Zero" (the foundation of the World Trade Center where the damage was most horrific) that most were turned away because the scene was becoming so congested.

In addition much has been done since September 11 to prepare for another attack. New York City and Washington, D.C., along with cities and towns throughout America, have revised their emergency-response plans to deal with increased threat of terrorist attack. Cities have spent millions of dollars on hiring, training, and equipping more firefighters, law enforcement officers, and medical personnel. The amounts being spent vary widely from state to state and city to city, as

Rescue workers in Charlotte, North Carolina, participate in a terrorism drill. Exercises like this have become common as cities prepare for the likelihood of a terrorist attack.

do the programs being funded. The most likely targets for terrorism, for example, vary widely in different states and cities, and therefore so do the measures being taken to protect them. As Gorman Freedberg of the *National Journal* reports: "In Florida, [safeguarding against terrorism] means paying special attention to protecting its Jewish population. In Illinois, it means tightly guarding its 11 nuclear reactors. And in Washington, D.C., it means trying to safeguard national landmarks."[5]

Despite these steps many critics feel that the government has not done nearly enough. In October 2002 the Council on Foreign Relations, a public policy think tank, sponsored an independent task force led by former Senators Gary Hart and Warren Rudman to evaluate U.S. homeland security efforts. The report concluded that: "America remains dangerously unprepared to prevent and respond to a catastrophic attack on U.S. soil. In all likelihood, the next attack will result in even greater casualties and widespread disruption to American lives and the economy."[6] The report charges that too many of the nation's first responders—firefighters, police, emergency medical providers, public works personnel and emergency management personnel—are underfunded, that too much of the nation's infrastructure is unguarded, and that there is little coordination among local, state, and federal agencies charged with homeland security. Stephen Flynn, who helped write the report, says: "We're not building the means to respond well. . . . When we have that next terrorist incident . . . the American people will be in disbelief about how little has been done."[7]

In a less ominous tone, Phil Anderson, head of the homeland security project at the Center for Strategic and International Studies in Washington, D.C., says, "We're safer, but we're not safe."[8] While it is impossible to protect every potential target, the nation is, for the most part, prepared to respond to conventional terrorist attacks—that is, bombings. As Ron Scherer of the *Christian Science Monitor* reports: "America has improved its ability to respond to World Trade

Center–size emergencies and smaller attacks."[9] However, many cities are not prepared to deal with potentially more devastating attacks using weapons of mass destruction.

Thus, the answer to the question—Is the United States prepared to respond to another terrorist attack?—is not a simple yes or no. It depends on many factors, including what type of attack America faces next, as well as where it occurs. "The truth is," writes *Time* writer Romesh Ratnesar, "we probably have no way of knowing whether the country is prepared for the next attack until after it occurs."[10] To this end the nation's first responders, as well as agencies at all levels of government, have been working to ensure a successful response to a possible future terrorist attack on America.

Chapter One

Protecting and Preparing

On September 11, 2001, armed only with small knives, nineteen al-Qaeda terrorists were able to hijack four aircraft, in one of the worst disasters in U.S. history. After the attacks an obvious first step was to make sure that terrorists could never again turn aircraft into guided missiles. To that end all cockpit doors on passenger aircraft were fortified to prevent intrusion. Airport baggage screeners were replaced with specially trained federal employees. Passengers became subjected to more thorough random searches. Air marshals—armed, specially trained agents of the Transportation Security Administration—were dispatched to ride aboard more flights. "I don't know if you're ever going to get a 100 percent secure system," says Dale Oderman, an aviation expert at Purdue University, "but we are definitely safer than we were."[11] Preventing another hijacking has become a priority.

Similarly a central part of U.S. homeland security strategy is a myriad of protective measures designed to make it so that the next attempted terrorist attack—whether a hijacking or something else—will fail. Homeland security experts agree that terrorists are unlikely to attempt a simple repeat of September 11 because many of the vulnerabilities—the so-called "holes"—in airline security have been addressed. Rather than targeting the airlines again, terrorists are more likely to search for other vulnerabilities to exploit. As the Bush administration's *National Strategy for Homeland Security*

A security guard displays a handheld computer that detects security breaches at airports. Using such devices is one way to protect against airport terrorist attacks.

explains: "Terrorists are opportunistic. They exploit vulnerabilities we leave exposed.... Increasing the security of a particular type of target, such as aircraft or buildings, makes it more likely that terrorists will seek a different target."[12] A fundamental part of homeland security, therefore, is the ongoing effort to identify and eliminate vulnerabilities before terrorists can take advantage of them. While the United States is preparing first responders and government agencies to respond to another attack, it is also taking steps to prevent such an attack from occurring in the first place.

Protecting Critical Infrastructure

Protecting critical infrastructure is a top priority of those charged with homeland security. The term *infrastructure* refers to the fundamental facilities that allow a town, a city, a state, or a nation to function. For example a city's critical infrastructure includes roads, power plants, electrical and phone lines, and water mains. The USA Patriot Act (the first major homeland security legislation passed after September 11) defines critical infrastructure as "systems and assets . . . so vital to the United States that the incapacity or destruction of such systems and assets would have a debilitating impact on security, national economic security, national public health or safety, or any combination of those matters."[13] A wide range of facilities—including America's transportation and communication networks; its ability to provide people with food, water, and power; and key economic and government centers—are all vital to the functioning of U.S. society.

The Department of Homeland Security (DHS) identifies thirteen critical infrastructure sectors worthy of protection. Among the most critical of these are agriculture, food, and water. The United States already has in place well-functioning food and water safety systems to protect against

Members of the National Guard patrol an airport in Maine. Following the September 11 attacks, the U.S. government passed legislation aimed at safeguarding America's infrastructure.

unintended contamination; the challenge for Homeland Security officials is to improve these systems' ability to protect against and respond to deliberate terrorist attempts at corruption through chemical or biological attack. Such attempts would not only inflict harm on individuals, but incite panic and cause long-term damage to the economy.

Some critical infrastructure sectors that need safeguarding are particularly vital for homeland security efforts. For example both first responders and state and federal governments depend heavily on the telecommunications sector, which includes phone, television, radio, and Internet services. The public health and emergency services sector is another key part of the nation's attack-response capability. A terrorist attack that damages or destroys a hospital or other public health facility could significantly reduce an area's ability to effectively respond.

Two critical infrastructures that are particularly hard to protect are energy and transportation. Protecting the energy sector involves guarding vulnerable dams and nuclear plants that generate electricity as well as oil and natural gas pipelines, while the transportation sector encompasses aviation, maritime traffic, ports, railroads, highways, trucking and busing, and public mass transit. The very size and diversity that make America's energy and transportation networks so vital to the nation's economy and national security also make these networks impossible to safeguard entirely.

Finally the attack on the World Trade Center showed that terrorists may hope to harm America's economy. Protecting the banking and finance sector involves not just physically guarding financial markets, banking operations, and major office buildings, but also ensuring that financial institutions and markets can quickly resume operations in the wake of an attack.

In addition to critical infrastructure, the federal government's homeland security strategy identifies another category—key assets—that encompasses noncritical structures and resources that may be likely targets for attack. Key assets

include sites that have symbolic importance, such as national monuments, tourist attractions, and centers of government and commerce, as well as sites where large numbers of people regularly congregate, such as sports stadiums. As Brian Michael Jenkins, an adviser to President Bush, says: "Targets offering high symbolic value or killing fields"[14] are particularly vulnerable to attack.

President Bush delivers a speech in February 2002 to gain support for a new budget that would allocate additional money for homeland security programs.

Security Strategies

Clearly, protecting the nation's critical infrastructure is no small task. The United States is home to countless potential terrorist targets, and security vulnerabilities abound. *U.S. News & World Report* writer Thomas Omestad warns that when infrastructure is concentrated in a small area, it makes things even worse. For example, "just 12 bridges across the Mississippi River are said to carry half of the nation's fiber-optic traffic. Just five feedlots supply virtually all of the nation's beef."[15] However, it would be impossible—and prohibitively expensive—to protect every potential target all the time. Instead, strategies have been developed to make the most use out of limited security resources. "We can't just do all, be all, for all," says police chief Joseph Samuels Jr. of Richmond, California, "but that which we choose to do, we want to do it well."[16]

One strategy is to make security as visible as possible, since terrorists are less likely to try to attack sites or smuggle weapons through areas that are obviously guarded. To this end there has been increased police presence at high-profile events such as the Super Bowl and the New Year's Eve celebration in New York City's Times Square, as well as at sporting events, parades, speeches, public gatherings, and special events. The hope is that the mere presence of law enforcement personnel will be enough to deter would-be terrorists.

Homeland Security director Tom Ridge (left) and other government officials listen as President Bush talks about his first meeting with the Homeland Security Council.

Another strategy is to make security efforts variable. For example air marshals are assigned to random flights so that terrorists cannot know in advance which flights are guarded and which are not. The overall goal is to ensure that terrorists cannot take advantage of security measures that are routine and unchanging. According to Tim Daniels, Missouri's Director of Homeland Security, studies of past al-Qaeda operations indicate that "they spend a lot of time on reconnaissance."[17] Much like a thief "casing" the building he plans to break into, it is believed that al-Qaeda operatives carefully study their targets and plan their attacks accordingly. U.S. intelligence authorities estimate that the September 11 attacks took years to plan. So, explains Daniels: "If they see police doing a roadblock in some place they've never seen [them] before, it's very disruptive to their plans."[18]

To further keep terrorists guessing, many of the specifics about U.S. vulnerabilities, and the security measures designed to protect them, are being guarded with more secrecy than before September 11. Public documents containing information about, or maps of, power plants, dams, gas and oil pipelines, chemical-storage sites, government buildings, and national monuments have been removed from government websites. And, in general, homeland security officials are hesitant to divulge specific information about attack-preparedness efforts and emergency-response plans so that terrorists cannot look for vulnerabilities in those efforts.

Sounding the Alarm

Again, however, a central tenet of homeland security measures is that, despite all the efforts being made to protect critical infrastructure and key assets, it is impossible to protect everything all the time. A terrorist attack may still be successful. Thus one of the most important parts of homeland security is the ability to quickly sound the alarm when a terrorist attack has taken place or is likely to occur.

Implementing a national warning system was one of the first steps that the federal government took after September 11. Homeland Security director, Tom Ridge, unveiled the advisory system in March 2002, well before the DHS was officially created. The advisory system designates five color-coded levels—ranging from green for "low" to red for "severe"—to inform federal agencies, state and local governments, and the public about possible terrorist threats.

However, for security purposes, the steps that are to be taken when the threat level is raised have only been described by the DHS in very general terms. At green alert, which indicates a low risk of attack, government agencies are advised to assess vulnerabilities in their jurisdictions. At blue alert, which indicates a general risk of attack, agencies are advised to review and update their emergency-response plans and keep the public informed. At yellow alert, which indicates an elevated risk of attack, authorities are to increase surveillance at critical locations and implement emergency-response plans. At orange alert, which indicates a high risk of attack, law enforcement authorities are to coordinate with the armed forces and increase precautions at public events. Government agencies are also advised to restrict their workforce to essential personnel. At red alert, which indicates a severe risk of attack, emergency personnel are to be mobilized, public transportation is to be curtailed, and public and government facilities are to be closed.

The steps to be taken at each alert level are so vague in part because, as DHS spokesperson, Brian Roehrkasse, explains: "There are too many different threats and potential scenarios for the government to offer anything other than such general precautions ahead of time."[19] Roehrkasse emphasizes that the Homeland Security Advisory System is primarily a way for the federal government to alert state and local homeland security agencies and that, in the event of an attack, the public should turn to local authorities first. For example Spenser Hsu of the *Washington Post* reports that: "Code Red won't be declared unless an attack occurs or is

President Bush inspects a chemical agent monitor, a tool that detects the presence of hazardous materials used to manufacture chemical weapons.

imminent, and that announcement will be intended mainly as a guide for the nation's homeland security agencies, government officials and such first responders as police and firefighters."[20]

Preparing the Public

While the Homeland Security Advisory System is designed to be most useful when an attack has occurred or is imminent, a number of other programs exists to provide more specific advice on how the general public can make their homes and families safer from terrorism. The American Red Cross, for example, offers disaster-preparedness classes around the country. The Department of Education has published a variety of preparedness materials for schools, and the DHS has launched www.ready.gov, an informational site that outlines

A Pentagon official demonstrates a gas mask and hazardous materials suit like those first responders would wear to protect themselves from a chemical or biological attack.

steps that offer advice on how individuals and families can prepare for an attack. The website offers information on making an emergency-preparedness kit, creating a family disaster plan, and special steps that individuals should take in the event of chemical, biological, or other attacks using weapons of mass destruction (WMD).

Other programs are designed to train members of the public to assist, or even act in place of, first responders. Citizen Corps, for example, helps coordinate volunteer activities that make communities safer and better prepared to respond to emergency situations. One of the programs that Citizen Corps helps coordinate is the Community Emergency Response Teams (CERT) program, which is run by the Federal Emergency Management Agency (FEMA). CERT members complete twenty hours of training on disaster preparedness, basic disaster medical operations, fire safety, light search and rescue, and other topics. Michael D. Brown, undersecretary of DHS Emergency Preparedness and Response, says: "Through the CERT program, citizens are better able to respond to an emergency or disaster. This is an essential way for citizens to help secure the homeland by supporting the work of our professional first responders."[21] In May 2003 the DHS announced that it would be providing $19 million in grants to strengthen the CERT program, an increase over the $17 million provided in 2002.

Preparing First Responders

The multitude of homeland preparedness measures that were taken around the country were so diverse that no single government agency could list them all. "Since September 11, even those who operate full-time in the field of domestic preparedness have found it difficult to keep track of the money, the programs, and the policies enacted in the flurry of activity,"[22] reports the Executive Session on Domestic Preparedness (ESDP), a government-sponsored task force. There are, however, some common themes in local preparedness efforts, most of which center around improving the capabilities of first responders.

To do their jobs effectively, first responders need the proper equipment and materials. Since the attacks of September 11, during which communications problems hampered some first responders, many cities have upgraded their first responders' communications networks. To prepare for chemical and biological attacks, communities stocked up on antibiotics, vaccines, chemical weapons antidotes, gas masks, and hazardous materials (hazmat) suits. Some also supply first responders with Geiger counters and other devices that can detect radiation.

Just as important as the equipment and supplies is the training to use them effectively. Before September 11, dealing with nuclear, radiological, chemical, and biological weapons was outside most first responders' purview. Now it has become part of the job. "Our mission has really expanded," says firefighter Steve Zomosky. The ESDP task force suggests that there should be a national standard for training in WMD:

> WMD response should be made part of the training that firefighters, police, HazMat (hazardous materials) workers, public health personnel, doctors, and nurses are required to complete before employment. While this instruction is conducted locally and is sometimes private, federal legislation should mandate that standards for training be set by the relevant federal agencies, and that training academies be trained directly by the federal experts.[23]

First responder training programs vary widely from state to state and city to city. A first step toward what ESDP suggests is the Weapons of Mass Destruction Certificate Program offered through the Internet by the U.S. Department of

Members of a hazmat team decontaminate each other after a drill simulating chemical attack. Emergency personnel across the country are beginning to participate in such first responder training exercises.

Justice, Center for Domestic Preparedness (CDP) in conjunction with American Military University. The CDP trains approximately twenty thousand first responders and homeland security planners annually in WMD preparedness at its site in Anniston, Alabama, and the online program is designed to reach thousands more. The five-part program focuses on the special threats posed by WMD attacks and the logistical challenges of coordinating all the different first responders and government agencies that respond to WMD attacks.

Simulated Attacks

Finally an integral part of first responders' attack preparedness is testing. Exercises in which emergency workers respond to simulated terrorist attacks can help spot weaknesses in both local emergency-response plans and in first responders' training. The largest full-scale drills that government agencies had ever staged to test their reactions to a terrorist attack was TOPOFF2, a series of exercises conducted in May 2003. Short for Top Officials 2, TOPOFF2 was a sequel to the original TOPOFF exercises conducted in May 2000. In TOPOFF2 a fictitious terrorist organization unleashed a two-pronged attack on Seattle and Chicago.

The TOPOFF2 drills began on Monday, May 12, with the mock explosion of a "dirty bomb" attack in Seattle. A dirty bomb is a regular bomb laced with harmful radioactive material. In the TOPOFF2 exercise, fake clouds of radiation were released into the surrounding area to simulate a dirty bomb's effect. The pretend explosion occurred near the city's Space Needle, in accordance with the expectation that terrorists will strike at high-profile targets. Plumes of smoke were released into the air, buses were overturned, and around 150 actors faked death or injury to simulate the devastation of the attack. Firefighters wearing protective gas masks decontaminated "victims" with water from fire hydrants before ambulances rushed them to nearby hospitals. The drill tested both Seattle's first responders and the federal DHS, as DHS director Ridge, organized a federal response to the mock attack. Canadian agencies also participated because of the proximity of Vancouver to the attack.

Then, on Thursday morning, May 14, Chicago first responders scrambled to deal with two more simulated catastrophes: the mock collapse of a building (responders found a real pile of rubble at the site of the pretend collapse) and the pretend release of harmful chemicals in suburban Chicago. Thursday night Chicago first responders dealt with over one hundred simulated casualties after the fictitious terrorist organization crashed a helicopter into a grounded Boeing 757 passenger jet.

Meanwhile, since Tuesday that same week, actors posing as patients had been reporting to Chicago hospitals complaining of fever, chills, and aches. By Thursday drill participants diagnosed the pretend ailment as bubonic plague. The TOPOFF2 exercises culminated late Thursday night in a raid on a make-believe biological lab in downtown Chicago that had been identified as the source of the epidemic. FBI units, along with Chicago SWAT (Special Weapons and Tactics) and Special Operations teams, raided the facility and decontaminated the site.

There were several lessons learned from the TOPOFF2 exercises. For example in Seattle some police officers rushed into the scene of the attack before the site was tested for radiation. In Chicago, homeland security officials learned how valuable volunteers can be in relieving overworked medical personnel by distributing medicines. "We push the envelope in these types of scenarios," says Ridge. "We push decision-making at all levels—local, state, and federal. . . . We look to uncover communication and coordination and other problems."[24]

Many states are performing similar exercises on a smaller scale. For example in May 2003 New York City's Office of Emergency Management administered a five-hour exercise called Operation Winter Sun. In the exercise over 250 actors posing as victims pretended to suffer the effects of chemical,

biological, or radiological attacks, testing first responders' ability to identify the effects of these types of attacks and decontaminate and treat victims. Seven hospitals and over seven hundred first responders participated in the exercise.

Rescue workers in Seattle respond to a simulated dirty bomb attack during the city's TOPOFF2 bioterrorism drill.

All these preparedness efforts are aimed at improving the nation's response to possible future terrorist attack. Until such an attack occurs, it is difficult to gauge which of these exercises and measures will be most effective. Ultimately, preparing to respond to unseen and unpredictable enemies is part of what homeland security is all about.

Chapter Two

The Basics of Emergency Response

President Dwight D. Eisenhower once remarked: "Plans are useless, but planning is indispensable."[25] Eisenhower, who had served as supreme commander of Allied forces in World War II, was referring to military battles when he made that comment. Military commanders routinely draw up detailed battle plans before engaging an enemy force, even though no battle ever goes exactly as planned. Surprises from enemy forces, equipment malfunctions, human error, and the general chaos of combat simply make it impossible to formulate a perfect battle plan. Nevertheless planning is essential. Using the accumulated wisdom gained from previous battles and wars, along with whatever (usually limited and imperfect) information is available about the enemy, good military commanders try to ensure that their troops are prepared to deal with the inevitable surprises of battle.

Homeland security efforts follow a similar approach, particularly the efforts that are being made to prepare for a possible future terrorist attack on U.S. soil. Terrorists have to their advantage the element of surprise. It is likely that there will be little or no prior warning of when, where, or how the next attack will occur. As in conventional warfare, the unpredictable nature of terrorism underscores the importance of planning even as it makes formulating a perfect attack-response plan impossible.

Terrorism and Emergency Response

The United States has relatively little experience in dealing with terrorist attacks; indeed, few American civilians were familiar with the concept of "homeland security" before the September 2001 attacks. The two major terrorist attacks prior to September 11 were the bombing of the basement of New York City's World Trade Center in February 1993, in which 6 people were killed, and the bombing of the Alfred P. Murrah Federal Building in downtown Oklahoma City in April 1995, in which 168 were killed. Homeland security planners are able to draw on the lessons that were learned in responding to these attacks as well as the attacks of September 11.

However, while the firefighters, police officers, and medical workers who responded to these terrorist attacks had, for the most part, little experience in responding to terrorist threats, these first responders were trained to deal with a wide variety of potential disasters of both natural and human origin. The planning and procedures that these cities had in

A soldier uses a portable computer to plan his strategy during a drill. Strategic planning is vital to the success of homeland security efforts.

place for general emergencies served them well when they were confronted with a terrorist attack. The challenge is to incorporate the possibility of a terrorist attack into these broader plans meant for dealing with emergencies such as fire, earthquake, explosion, or flood.

By placing U.S. terrorism-response plans in a broader context, homeland security planners take advantage of the fact that most cities are already familiar with the basic steps that must be taken in response to a disaster. As a report on homeland security from Harvard University's John F. Kennedy School of Government explains, cities' attack-response plans should not try to reinvent the wheel:

Miami firefighters participate in a terrorist attack drill. Local rescue workers like these had little experience with terrorist activity before September 11, 2001.

> There is no benefit, and potentially much harm, in adopting new programs when old ones will do. Although the terrorism threat is evolving continuously, many of the existing practices and policies of first responders can be utilized to assist in homeland security.[26]

The existing practices and policies the report refers to center around several areas that are key to emergency response regardless of the type of emergency. In very broad terms these areas are communications, mass medical care, protective actions, and recovery.

Communication is one of the most important—and most overlooked—elements of emergency response. There are two critical types of communication that must be preserved in the event of a terrorist attack: (1) the ability of public officials to inform the public, and (2) the ability of first responders to communicate with each other in order to coordinate their efforts.

Informing the Public

The first type of communication—informing the public—is vital to avoid panic. FEMA explains that:

> Terrorism is designed to be catastrophic. The intent of a terrorist attack is to cause maximum destruction of lives and property; create chaos, confusion, and public panic; and stress local, State, and Federal response resources. Accurate and timely information, disseminated to the public and media immediately and often over the course of the response, is vital to minimize accomplishment of these terrorist objectives.[27]

An effective emergency-response plan must therefore address how emergency information will be disseminated to the public.

The mass media—primarily television and radio—are the most reliable and productive ways for first responders and government officials to inform the public. Maintaining good relationships with the media is a regular part of state and local emergency management offices' operations. "With 24-hour news," writes Frances Edward-Winslow, director of emergency preparedness for the city of San Jose, California, "it is possible to provide life-saving information to many

A man protects his house with plastic wrap in response to a heightened terror alert. Improving communication with the public is one way the U.S. government is trying to protect the country from terrorist attack.

community members in a short period of time, and often in multiple languages." [28]

This was certainly the case on September 11, 2001. While the media reported on a few false alarms in the first few hours of the coverage that day, for the most part the nation's television and radio networks kept the public informed and helped avert panic. The major television networks covered the attacks around the clock, and many cable networks suspended their own programming in favor of covering the developments in New York City and Washington, D.C. In the weeks and months after the attacks, some pundits criticized cable news channels for their nonstop postattack coverage of September 11. However, most agreed that, on the day of the attack, they provided a major public service. "Journalists are first responders," asserts Randy Atkins, a senior media relations officer for the National Academy of Engineering. "Not only do they sometimes get to the scene first, but they are the only ones focused on and able to describe the level of risk to the public. They can save lives through the efficient delivery of good information." [29]

Many news agencies developed emergency-response plans to help reporters respond to possible future attacks. Newspapers and magazines such as *USA Today* and *U.S. News & World Report* have contingency plans to meet at backup newsrooms in the event that access to their main offices is disrupted. Journalists' safety is also a concern. "WNBC-TV in New York has outfitted most of its news vehicles with nuclear, biological, and chemical kits that contain protective body suits, gas masks, gloves, booties, tape, and water," reports Rachel Smolkin in *American Journalism Review*, and "CBS News, based in midtown Manhattan, has provided protective body suits, gas masks and escape hoods, as well as training in their use, to crews, producers and correspondents in major U.S. cities."[30]

Communication Among First Responders

The second type of key emergency communication—first responders keeping each other informed and coordinating their efforts—is one of the greatest challenges facing emergency-response planners. Public policy professor Viktor Mayer-Schönberger provides a vivid illustration of the challenges faced by law enforcement officers and other emergency personnel who responded to the April 1999 Columbine High School shootings, in which two students shot fifteen students and teachers and wounded dozens more. During that disaster, first responders did not know how many attackers they faced or what the attackers' goals were. Screaming students were fleeing the school; others were wounded and needed medical attention. Mayer-Schönberger writes:

> Yet as it turned out, the biggest challenge on that Tuesday afternoon was not battling the two attackers.... The biggest challenge was coordinating heavily armed and ready-to-fire police forces from half a dozen sheriff's offices and twenty area police departments, forty-six ambulances, and two helicopters from twelve fire and EMS agencies, as well as personnel from a number of state and federal agencies.[31]

The problem, explains Mayer-Schönberger, was fundamentally a technical one. Different agencies—local police, state police, firefighters, and others—each used different radio systems. The cellular phone network became overloaded as hundreds of journalists and first responders converged on the scene. Responders essentially had no way of communicating other than face-to-face. "The real miracle of Columbine High," says Mayer-Schönberger, "is that nobody else got killed because of the complete communications breakdown, either through friendly fire or uncoordinated agency activity."[32]

Similar communications breakdowns occurred during the 1993 World Trade Center bombing, the 1995 Oklahoma City bombing, and the September 11 attacks. In Manhattan on September 11, for example, intercommunication between police made them aware of some dangers that firefighters were not. More effective communications systems could have saved lives. As Dale Craig reported in the *Journal of Counterterrorism and Homeland Security*:

> Police helicopters circling the World Trade Center on September 11th, for example, could see that the first tower was on the brink of collapse. While those in the helicopter could communicate with police units on the ground they were unable to talk directly to the firemen and others inside the building to warn them of the impending catastrophe.[33]

And in Washington, D.C., emergency workers from ten different jurisdictions arrived to help victims of the attack on the Pentagon—but because they used different radio frequencies, their efforts were initially marred by confusion and delay. Ultimately, says Arlington County fire chief, Edward P. Plaugher: "We relied on communications technology perfected by the ancient Greeks: carrying messages on foot."[34]

Each of these incidents demonstrated the need for interoperability—the linking of communications networks among different emergency agencies. By 2003 most cities and towns still did not have fully interoperable communications sys-

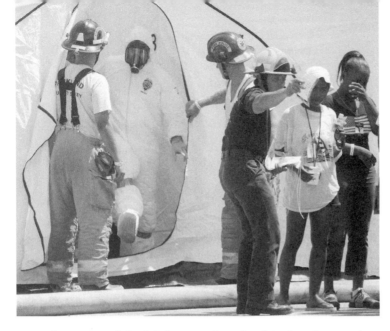

Firefighters and EMTs participate in a 2003 terrorism drill. These men belong to one of the many agencies in Florida that worked together to test their communications systems.

tems because of the high costs involved in implementing them. "According to some estimates," reports Craig, "it would cost up to $500 million for a major metropolitan area like Los Angeles to convert all of the current radios used by its fire, police, and emergency workers to a single network."[35]

A wide variety of solutions has been proposed to make first responders' communications systems interoperable, some involving satellite uplinks, digital radio systems, cellular phone carriers, and wireless computer networks. In addition to cost a major challenge is getting so many different emergency units to adopt a common set of technologies and protocols that would help them to act in concert. Homeland security officials agree that universally accepted operability standards and equipment are needed, but such standards may take years to implement.

Mass Medical Care

In the meantime one thing that is certain is that in the event of an attack, many people will need basic emergency medical services (EMS). One of the first things that any emergency-response plan must address is how to provide EMS as quickly as possible to those who need it. For smaller-scale emergencies, medical services are generally provided by paramedics and emergency medical technicians (EMTs) who treat victims at the scene and during transport to local hospitals via ground or air ambulances. Emergency care is then provided according to the hospital's normal procedures. Throughout the country variations on this general system have been tested by countless automobile crashes, fires, and other emergencies.

The main concern is that a terrorist attack could overwhelm a community's EMS capabilities. For small-scale terrorist incidents, conventional EMS is likely to be adequate. If a car bomb injured dozens of people, for example, the EMS response, at the scene and at the hospital, might not be very different than for a serious traffic accident. Likewise EMS resources in New York City and Washington, D.C., were able to respond effectively to the September 11 attacks. (The

Health Department officials in Illinois distribute mock medication to volunteers during a drill aimed at preparing EMS workers for a terrorist attack.

extreme violence of the World Trade Center collapse left relatively few survivors with serious injuries.)

Homeland security experts warn, however, that normal EMS procedures could be inadequate for large-scale terrorist attacks. Few physicians have handled true disasters—incidents in which hundreds or thousands of people with severe or unique injuries strain available medical resources. "A true mass casualty situation is not like your typical Saturday night influx of multiple casualties into an urban trauma center," cautions Eric R. Frykberg, a surgeon at the University of Florida. "There are certain things you have to change in your approach, and it's important for surgeons and trauma experts to be aware of that."[36]

When Resources Are Overwhelmed

One concern is that a hospital's resources could be overwhelmed fairly quickly. Since the early 1990s, in order to curb the rising costs of health care, hospitals have been working to reduce unnecessary spending. The result is that many hospitals have enough resources to handle day-to-day operations but not much more. "Hospital emergency departments are now commonly filled to capacity during daily operations and must divert even critically ill emergency cases,"[37] writes a group of physicians for *UF News*.

The most common solution to what emergency medical planners refer to as "surges" in demand for medical services is to divert patients to other hospitals. An effective emergency-response plan designates not just which hospitals are to be the main destinations for attack victims, but also the network of hospitals and trauma centers that will serve as secondary destinations for EMS personnel.

But in a large-scale attack, an entire area's medical resources could be quickly overwhelmed. Over the course of hours and days, victims can be transported to out-of-area medical facilities, and agencies such as the Red Cross can set up mass-care facilities to supplement area medical services.

But in the crucial first minutes and hours after an attack, medical first responders must change their normal approach. As Frykberg explains:

> Typically, in everyday medical care, everyone who's injured goes to the hospital, and we use our maximum resources on each patient.... The challenge in a mass casualty situation is in keeping most patients out of the hospital, not bringing them in. A change in mindset has to occur. Otherwise it will overwhelm the hospital's ability to sort out the relatively few injuries that need major treatment from the tremendous number that don't. If you don't handle it properly, existing evidence clearly shows this can lead to unnecessary loss of lives.[38]

This process of sorting victims by immediacy of treatment needed is known as triage. In triage EMS personnel must quickly decide which victims need first aid immediately and which can wait, which victims should be first to be taken to the hospital, and which patients can be saved and which cannot. Such life-and-death decisions are more associated with wartime battlefields than with civilian emergencies, and in fact homeland security planners may look to the military for lessons in how to deal with massive casualties.

Large-scale emergency response becomes even more complicated in the event of a WMD attack involving chemical, biological, or radiological weapons. Whereas in a conventional bombing most of the destruction is limited to the initial explosion, WMD attacks can become more destructive over time as more people are exposed to the hazardous substance(s) in question.

Depending on the type of weapon, EMS personnel may need to decontaminate affected individuals in order to remove the hazardous substance from the victim and keep it from spreading to others (including the EMS personnel themselves). According to the Council on Foreign Relations, many hospitals are ill-equipped to deal with a WMD attack. "Even a [major] trauma center like Boston Medical Center, which

Officers in a SWAT unit rappel from a helicopter to practice aerial evacuation procedures. In the event of a terrorist attack, efficient evacuation procedures are essential to safeguarding lives.

is certified to treat the most serious injuries around the clock, can only decontaminate about 20 patients at a time."[39]

Decontamination procedures will vary depending on the hazardous substance in question. Exposure to radiation, for example, requires specific types of treatment, while a bioterror incident could involve infectious diseases that should be met with immunizations and possible quarantines. EMS and hospital personnel must train and prepare for each of the various responses to different WMD so they can ascertain what types of specialized treatment attack victims will need.

Decontamination is what FEMA calls a protective action—an umbrella term that refers to many different steps that first responders may take to minimize casualties at the scene of attack. While decontamination is an appropriate protective action for several types of WMD attacks, there is one protective action that could be applied to almost any major terrorist attack: evacuation.

Evacuations

On the most basic level, evacuation involves simply getting people away from danger. Small-scale evacuations are an integral part of attack response. Particularly in the event of a biological, chemical, or radiological attack, officials would almost certainly require people to evacuate the immediate area in which the hazardous substance was released. Larger-scale evacuations, however, are much more difficult. There are enormous challenges involved in evacuating all but the smallest cities in the United States.

Emergency planners can point to plenty of real-life examples that demonstrate the logistical nightmares that evacuations entail. For example, Johanna Neuman, of the *Los Angeles Times*, notes that: "In Florida in 1999, 2.5 million people hit the highways to escape Hurricane Floyd—at least 1 million more than authorities expected."[40] The evacuation resulted in massive traffic jams. Some motorists were stuck in their cars for ten hours on stretches of interstate that normally take two to three hours to traverse. With 2.5 million evacuees, the Hurricane Floyd evacuation was the largest in U.S. history. In comparison the Census Bureau estimates that 8 million people live in New York City (1.5 million in Manhattan alone); 3.7 million live in Los Angeles; and 2.9 million live in Chicago. Evacuating such large numbers of people in a short period of time may simply be impossible.

For an evacuation to be successful, local authorities require the cooperation of those being evacuated. As a Red Cross attack-readiness pamphlet explains: "If local authorities ask you to leave your home, they have a good reason to make this request, and you should heed the advice immediately. Listen to your radio or TV, follow the instructions of local emergency officials."[41] However, there are a variety of

Police officers in Washington, D.C., participate in an evacuation drill. For a successful evacuation, authorities require the full cooperation of the people being evacuated.

Office workers flee the Pentagon on September 11, 2001. Following the attack, local agencies coordinated efforts to improve evacuation procedures in Washington, D.C.

reasons that some people may choose not to evacuate immediately. One consideration is parents' concern for their children. For example, as Neuman asks: "If parents are instructed to head north while their children are at a school to the south, will they obey a police officer's order?"[42] Another concern is pets. Many pet owners consider their pets family and will not leave them behind, but evacuee shelters set up by the Red Cross and other agencies often refuse to accept animals. On an individual level these concerns may seem reasonable, but on a city-wide scale individuals' personal priorities could foil authorities' efforts to orchestrate a timely evacuation.

All these potential problems mean that large-scale evacuation is an option of last resort for most cities. Nevertheless it is an option to be used in certain scenarios. According to Don Jacks of FEMA: "Evacuation is still the primary protective measure in the event of a nuclear incident."[43] If terrorists ever threatened to attack with a nuclear weapon—a scenario that is considered highly unlikely—evacuation might be the protective action that would save the most lives.

For security reasons most states and cities keep their evacuation plans secret. One exception is the District of Columbia that, since September 11—according to Neuman—has become a model of emergency planning: "In the event of an emergency, traffic lights are to be synchronized between Washington and its feeder suburbs in Virginia and Maryland. The city has installed 750 signs showing motorists the way out."[44]

Search-and-Rescue Operations

Once the attack itself is over, the focus of emergency response shifts to recovery. For conventional attacks the critical first phase of recovery is search and rescue. Emergency workers differentiate between light and heavy search-and-rescue operations. "Light search and rescue operations are designed to provide an initial search . . . to locate victims with minor or no injuries and help them exit from lightly damaged [disaster areas],"[45] states a Los Angeles County fact sheet. Light search-and-rescue operations are often conducted by firefighters, but other emergency workers and even average citizens may lead or assist in light search-and-rescue efforts.

Heavy search-and-rescue operations involve locating, rescuing, and the initial medical stabilization of persons trapped in hard-to-reach spaces. Members of heavy search-and-rescue units are trained in emergency medicine and may include physicians. Members of search-and-rescue teams also possess an understanding of engineering, construction, and structural design. Such knowledge is vital in identifying both potential air pockets within collapsed buildings and parts of the buildings that may still be unstable. Canines can be part of these teams as well. In New York City after September 11, specially trained search-and-rescue dogs equipped with cameras, microphones, and infrared sensors capable of detecting body heat were used to search small air pockets for survivors.

Search equipment may include common building supplies such as concrete saws, jackhammers, drills, lumber, and rope, which are used to safely and slowly remove victims from the rubble. Other search tools are becoming increasingly high tech. As a FEMA report describes: "Snake-like cameras and fiber-optic scopes are used to locate victims trapped in rubble. Sensitive listening devices that can detect even the slightest human sound locate victims who are still alive."[46] Heavy search-and-rescue units may make use of construction vehicles if necessary, or of helicopters to provide the search team with an aerial view of the search area. Generators, lights, radios, cellular phones, and laptop computers may be used to maintain communications during a search.

Search-and-rescue units also have medical equipment and supplies available and are usually supported by a logistics section that provides the unit with the resources necessary to work around the clock—for example, cots, food and water, and cold-weather gear. The longest that earthquake victims trapped beneath collapsed buildings are known to have ever survived is thirteen days, so search-and-rescue efforts typically continue for at least two weeks.

Providing for Victims' Physical and Psychological Needs

Other recovery measures include finding food, water, and shelter for attack victims whose homes might have been destroyed. State and local governments, or organizations such as the Red Cross and the Salvation Army, may set up emergency shelters to meet these needs. The public can also play an important role here. For example, after September 11, many communities set up emergency call centers and others expanded their "211" services. People can call 211 to access health and human services information in the event of an emergency; they can also volunteer to help others. United Way president, Brian Gallagher, says that in the days after September 11, when hundreds of travelers were stranded at Hartsdale Airport in Atlanta, "Residents of Atlanta started calling 211 offering their own homes for people to stay and they were connected to people who needed help."[47]

Once the physical needs of attack victims have been addressed, emergency-response officials can turn to the psychological and emotional consequences of the attack. Terrorist attacks, by their nature, traumatize more than just their immediate victims. As a report from the Harvard University John F. Kennedy School of Government notes: "While the 2001 attacks on the World Trade Center and the Pentagon resulted in thousands of deaths and physical injuries, the psychological casualties numbered in the tens to hundreds of thousands. . . . Indeed, these psychological effects are integral to the 'success' of terrorist actions."[48] The Red Cross includes mental health services as part of its overall efforts to help communities that have suffered a disaster.

As in every stage of emergency response, communications are critical. A well-informed public is more capable of coping with the natural fears that accompany an attack than a population that is left to guess about what threats are imminent. A continuous stream of calm, timely public information is necessary to begin managing the long-term consequences of a terrorist attack. It is at this stage that the work of emergency responders ends and the work of local, state, and national leaders begins.

Emergency-response officials tend to the needs of victims during a bioterrorism drill in Seattle.

Chapter Three

Nuclear and Radiological Attacks

I n discussions of homeland security, the term *weapons of mass destruction* (WMD) is used to encompass chemical, biological, nuclear, and radiological weapons, and to differentiate between these types of weapons and conventional weapons such as guns and bombs. There are two main reasons that homeland security experts are so concerned about the possibility of WMD terrorist attacks. First, as the term suggests, WMD are potentially much more dangerous than conventional arms. Second, the threat of a WMD attack requires very different preparations than those being made for conventional attacks (and the different types of WMD attacks each require different preparations). These two considerations underlie the U.S. homeland security strategy surrounding WMD threats.

Low Probability, High Consequence

Many homeland security experts believe that the likelihood of a WMD terrorist attack is very low—or at least much lower than the likelihood of a conventional attack. This is because WMD are harder to obtain or build than conventional firearms and explosives. "There are a limited number of terrorist movements in the world, only a few of which have the ability and desire to acquire and use [weapons of mass destruction],"[49] states a report from the ESDP. Similarly no terrorist group is believed to have the materials necessary to build nuclear weapons.

To help put the risks in perspective, consider that, world-wide, there has never been a terrorist incident involving nuclear or radiological weapons—in contrast to scores of bombings, aircraft hijackings, and hostage takings since the 1970s. As Harvey Kushner, an expert on terrorism at Long Island University, puts it: "Terrorists have killed many people with conventional weaponry—not some James Bond–type device."[50]

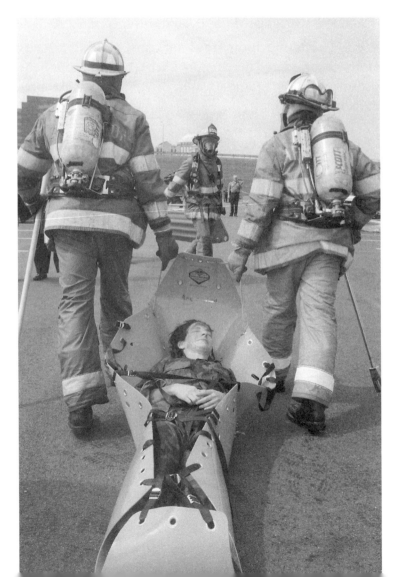

Although a WMD attack in the United States is unlikely, emergency personnel, like these firefighters, continue to train for the possibility.

While the likelihood of a severe WMD terrorist incident is very low, nuclear and radiological weapons are nevertheless major homeland security concerns. The reason for this, explains the ESDP report, is based on simple prudence:

> It is an issue the government cannot ignore. The consequences of a successful [WMD] attack would be severe. Advances in [technology] raise the destructive potential of a single terrorist act. Therefore, even a small WMD incident should be treated extremely seriously.... Terrorism with weapons of mass destruction should therefore be seen as a *low-probability* but *high-consequence* threat.[51]

While a bombing or other type of conventional terrorist attack is considered much more likely, the enormous dangers of a major WMD attack are a driving force in U.S. preparedness efforts.

Assessing the Nuclear Threat

Nuclear bombs are the most destructive weapons known and are therefore appealing to terrorist groups, whose goal is to spread fear and panic through destruction. As WMD researchers Graham Allison and Andrei Kokoshin report: "There is no doubt that Osama bin Laden and his associates have serious nuclear ambitions. For almost a decade they have been actively seeking nuclear weapons, and, as President Bush has noted, they would use such weapons against the United States or its allies 'in a heartbeat.'"[52] The prospect of terrorists actually acquiring nuclear weapons is a nightmarish, but unlikely, scenario. There are three ways that terrorists might acquire nuclear weapons: stealing them, illegally buying them, or building them.

Only eight countries are known to have nuclear weapons: the United States, Russia, Great Britain, France, China, Israel, India, and Pakistan. Iran and North Korea are also believed to have active nuclear weapons development programs. The weapons arsenals of Britain, China, France, Israel, and the

United States are considered to be well protected. India's and Pakistan's nuclear arsenals are thought to be less secure, in part because the nuclear weapons programs in those countries are relatively new, and the security measures surrounding them are not as well developed.

The security surrounding nuclear weapons and material in Russia and other former Soviet republics is of greatest concern. Prior to its collapse in 1991, the Soviet Union possessed a nuclear arsenal that rivaled that of the United States. Since 1991, however, Russia and many other former Soviet republics have experienced economic turmoil, crime, and government corruption. Although there is no evidence of missing nuclear weapons, some of the Soviet military's armaments have been, and continue to be, sold on the black market. There have also been several attempted thefts of the materials needed to power a nuclear explosion in the former Soviet Union. In December 1998 Russian authorities

A nuclear terrorist attack, like this simulated attack on a nuclear facility near Las Vegas, would be devastating to the United States.

announced they had foiled a plot to steal forty-one pounds of such material at a weapons plant about one thousand miles east of Moscow, and in August 2002 U.S., Russian, and Serbian forces raided a site in Belgrade, the capital of Serbia and Montenegro, and seized over 100 pounds of uranium.

Theft of nuclear devices from India, Pakistan, and Russia is a significant threat that the international community is working to reduce. In addition the concern that foreign gov-

South Koreans burn the North Korean flag to protest North Korea's nuclear program. Nuclear weapons programs in North Korea, Russia, and other politically unstable countries are of great concern to the United States.

ernments hostile to the United States or its allies might develop nuclear weapons and supply or sell them to terrorists has become a major foreign policy issue. (The belief that Iraq was engaged in the development of nuclear weapons was one of the reasons behind the U.S. invasion of that country in 2003.)

Terrorists seeking to build a nuclear bomb would need to procure weapons-grade uranium or plutonium—the materials that fuel the bomb's explosive nuclear reaction. In general, the more uranium or plutonium, the more destructive the bomb. These fissile materials, while still relatively difficult to obtain, are more widely available than nuclear weapons themselves. Both uranium and plutonium are used as fuel in nuclear reactors around the world. Bob Port of the *New York Daily News* reports that: "More than 22 tons of highly enriched uranium are controlled by civilians in some 245 aging nuclear power plants and research reactors in as many as 58 countries."[53] Japan, Russia, India, and several European states also reprocess spent reactor fuel, extracting bomb-grade plutonium in the process. Securing the fissile material at these sites is one of the top priorities in the international effort to prevent nuclear terrorism. Despite the security challenges, says Matthew Bunn, a researcher for Harvard's Managing the Atom project, "We have no evidence that any nuclear materials are yet in the hands of terrorists."[54]

Horrific Consequences

If terrorists procure the necessary fissile material, they might be able to build a crude nuclear device. The basic technical information needed to construct such a device is widely available, as is the necessary equipment. Smuggling such a weapon into the United States would be difficult but far from impossible, and once inside the country, detecting the weapon would be a challenge. In many cities sensors are being deployed that can detect radioactive emissions, but the sensors have limited range and lead shields can hide a bomb's emissions.

The Department of Energy (DOE) also maintains Nuclear Emergency Search Teams whose purpose is to locate radioactive weapons or materials should they enter the United States. Operating in secret in America's major cities, these teams act largely on leads from federal intelligence agencies.

If terrorists were able to launch a successful nuclear attack, the devastation could be almost inconceivable. Within the first few seconds of a nuclear blast, the explosion emits an intense burst of light and heat that will blind, burn, and set fire to anyone or anything in the blast radius. The burst of energy also results in an air-pressure shockwave that moves outward from the blast site at supersonic speeds, sending people and objects flying. The explosion produces initially high levels of ionizing radiation that cause death within a few weeks to those exposed.

In Hiroshima, one of the Japanese cities on which the United States used nuclear bombs at the end of World War II, the fires from the blast coalesced into a firestorm. The oxygen rushing into the many building fires fed the flames until everything in the area had been consumed. In the weeks and years after the explosion, residual radioactivity in the form of fallout caused cancer, birth defects, and other maladies in those exposed to it. An estimated one hundred thousand deaths at Hiroshima resulted from radiation sickness—far more than the roughly forty-five thousand who were killed in the initial blast.

The exact effect of a nuclear blast on an American city would depend on a number of factors, including the power of the blast, the population density, the local terrain, and the prevailing weather conditions.

The Council on Foreign Relations estimates that a relatively small nuclear blast in midtown Manhattan would kill more than two hundred thousand people, and radioactive fallout that would follow could kill half the exposed population as far as three miles away within a few weeks. A larger blast could kill millions.

A Focus on Prevention

It is difficult to imagine the effects that this type of devasta-tion would have on the United States. The potential damage that nuclear weapons could cause is so great that, more so than for any other type of terrorist threat, the homeland secu-rity strategy regarding nuclear weapons is one of attack pre-vention rather than attack response. Allison and Kokoshin write:

Soldiers in the U.S. Strategic Command patrol Nebraska's Offutt Air Force Base. These soldiers help secure and protect America's nuclear weapons.

> Nuclear terrorism is largely a preventable disaster. The good news about nuclear terrorism can be summarized in one line: no highly enriched uranium or plutonium, no nuclear explosion, no nuclear terrorism. Though the world's stockpiles of nuclear weapons and weapons-usable materials are vast, they are finite.... While challenging, a specific program of actions to keep nuclear materials out of the hands of the most dangerous groups is not beyond reach.[55]

The United States has spearheaded several nuclear security initiatives, working closely with Russia in agreeing to cut nuclear deployments and providing funding to help improve security at nuclear sites. In 1992 the United States also began paying Russia to dilute its uranium to less than 20 percent enrichment, which is less than weapons grade but still enough for use as fuel in nuclear reactors. At the June 2002 G8 summit—a meeting of the world's eight most economically influential nations—the United States, along with Canada, France, Germany, Italy, Japan, Russia, and the United Kingdom, pledged $20 billion to secure Russian nuclear materials. At the June 2003 G8 summit, those nations issued a joint declaration denouncing the nuclear weapons programs of North Korea and Iran.

Although they are grim, homeland security officials have considered nuclear attack–response scenarios. In terms of evacuation, fires, destroyed buildings, and massive casual-

Although emergency personnel continue to train to respond to nuclear attack, the best way to safeguard against nuclear terrorism is to keep nuclear materials out of the hands of terrorists.

ties, the response to a nuclear attack might be similar to that of a very large scale conventional attack. Hundreds of thousands of people might require urgent medical care; in the longer term, tens of thousands would need shelter. The key distinction between a nuclear attack and a large-scale conventional bombing would be the effects of radiation. Radiation would also be the key element in two other types of threats: attacks using radiological bombs and attacks on nuclear facilities.

Radiation as a Weapon

Nuclear bombs cause devastation through both the initial high-energy explosion and the ionizing radiation—known as fallout—that lingers after the blast. However, because the fissile materials required to build a nuclear bomb are difficult to acquire, terrorists are thought to be more likely to attack with a radiological dispersion device (RDD). An RDD is a combination of conventional explosives and radioactive material designed to scatter radioactive materials throughout an area.

Radiation is a form of energy generated by atoms as they undergo internal changes. Ionizing radiation is a high-energy form of radiation that can be harmful to humans because it causes charged particles to form in the cells it encounters. Ionizing radiation can strip electrons from the living tissue in human bodies. At low levels this may cause the development of cancer in those tissues. Moderately high levels of radiation (four hundred to one thousand times those that people are exposed to each year) may cause radiation sickness, a condition marked by nausea, vomiting, hair loss, and serious blood disorders. Very high levels of radiation, such as those produced by a nuclear explosion, are extremely lethal.

RDDs, also known as dirty bombs, would be much easier for terrorists to build than nuclear devices. Assembling a dirty bomb would not be much harder than assembling a conventional bomb, since the simplest dirty bombs are just conventional explosives laced with radioactive material. And RDDs do not require the special fissile materials used in nuclear bombs—any harmful radioactive material might be used, in amounts as small as half a cup. "Two of the most common radiological sources that might be used in such a bomb are cobalt 60 and cesium 137," Bill Nichols, Mimi Hall, and Peter Eisner report in *USA Today.* "Both are used in medical equipment, such as X-ray machines, and food-irradiation plants." [56]

Attacks on Nuclear Facilities

In addition to the threat of radiological bombs, terrorists might try to attack one of America's 103 nuclear power plants with conventional explosives, hoping to disperse lethal radiation into the surrounding area. This would be a type of radiological attack, one that uses radiation from the reactor as a weapon. Reactors are not particularly vulnerable targets. With sixteen-foot-thick concrete walls, barbed wire, surveillance cameras, motion sensors, and armed response teams, they are designed to be durable and disaster proof. But neither are they completely invulnerable. As David Kyd of the International Atomic Energy Agency notes, reactors "are built to withstand impacts, but not that of a wide-bodied passenger jet full of fuel. A deliberate hit of that sort is something that was never in any scenario at the design stage. . . . The consequences of a direct hit could be catastrophic." [57]

Aside from the reactor itself, terrorists might also try to explode the spent radioactive fuel that some plants store outside their containment buildings. "A lot of the spent nuclear fuel casks can be hit with a shoulder-fired missile by someone standing outside the fence," [58] says Dave Lochbaum, nuclear safety engineer at the Union of Concerned Scientists. Terrorists could also target nuclear waste material as it is transported by rail and truck.

Soldiers guard a nuclear reactor in 2003. Concerns that terrorists might attack nuclear reactors caused the government to increase security at nuclear power plants across the United States.

Security measures at nuclear sites have certainly improved in the wake of September 11. For example one of the first steps the Nuclear Regulatory Commission took was to double, from five to ten, the number of security guards that are required to be on duty at each reactor. The DOE also decided to move part of the Los Alamos National Laboratory, which performs research on nuclear energy and nuclear safeguards, from New Mexico to a remote area of the Nevada desert. However, as with other potential terrorist targets, it may be impossible to make America's nuclear facilities completely safe from terrorism.

Responding to Radiological Attacks

Decontamination—removing contaminated clothes and washing the skin and hair—would be the first step in treating victims of radiation exposure. Potassium iodide, a type of salt, can help reduce the risk of development of thyroid cancer as a result of radiation exposure. After September 11 some hospitals began stockpiling the substance, and the government distributed potassium iodide pills to residents living within ten miles of a nuclear reactor. However there is no cure for radiation exposure. Physicians can only treat the symptoms. In fact relatively little is known about radiation sickness, and most of the data on the condition comes from survivors of the bombs dropped on Hiroshima and Nagasaki in 1945.

Low levels of radiation, such as those likely to be produced by a dirty bomb, would have little immediate effect and are mostly dangerous in the long term. Increased risk of cancer would be the main consequence for those exposed. Educating the public about the relative dangers presented by different levels of radiation—either as a preparedness measure or as part of the response to an attack—is vital to reducing the panic that could accompany a radiological attack.

A firefighter is hosed down in a decontamination center. Decontamination is the first step in treating people exposed to radiation.

"The truth is, you have to start out with a boatload of radioactive material in a dirty bomb for the health risk to the population to be significant," says Jonathan Links of the Johns Hopkins School of Public Health. "The real threat of a dirty bomb is psychological."[59]

Depending on the amount and type of radioactive material used, radioactive fallout from a nuclear or radiological attack could linger in an area for weeks, years, or even decades, potentially rendering large urban areas uninhabitable. In addition Federation of American Scientists president, Henry Kelly, notes that: "There are often no effective ways to decontaminate buildings that have been exposed at these levels."[60] Recovery from a nuclear or radiological attack could, therefore, include demolition of important commercial and government centers or even historic landmarks. Kelly has testified before Congress that a dirty bomb attack in New York City "would result in losses of potentially trillions of dollars."[61]

Evacuation and Sheltering

In the event of a radiological attack, or in the aftermath of a nuclear attack, protecting the public from radioactive fallout will be a primary concern. Officials would likely implement evacuation plans, especially if the radioactive fallout is confined to a small area. To aid in evacuation first responders can call on the Defense Threat Reduction Agency (DTRA), which operates the Hazard Prediction Assessment Capability (HPAC) computer program. HPAC is capable of predicting where radioactive fallout will move. DTRA spokesperson, Robert Bennett, says the program "considers weather conditions along with radiological factors. It can show you what will happen in twenty minutes, then forty minutes, and so on."[62] HPAC was used to track the asbestos particles released from the structures destroyed on September 11.

Emergency workers may also direct people to designated fallout shelters. In the 1950s and 1960s, when the United

A mother and her children practice running to an underground fallout shelter in 1961. Many such shelters were built during the 1950s and 1960s to provide protection from radioactive fallout particles.

States was bracing for a possible nuclear attack from the Soviet Union, many cities and towns designated the basements of some public and private buildings as fallout shelters. However, according to the Department of Homeland Security (DHS), an effective fallout shelter "can be any protected space, provided that the walls and roof are thick enough to absorb the radiation given off by fallout particles."[63]

There are three factors that increase a fallout shelter's effectiveness. The first is shielding. According to the DHS, "the more heavy, dense, materials—thick walls, concrete, bricks, books and earth—between you and the fallout particles, the better."[64] The second is distance. The farther the shelter is from the fallout particles, the better. The third is time. Fallout shelters should be able to support their inhabitants for up to two weeks, after which the radiation will have dramatically decreased.

Preventing Worst-Case Scenarios

A terrorist attack with nuclear or radiological weapons, however unlikely, would no doubt be the most devastating event that the United States has ever faced. Such weapons truly present homeland security officials with some of the worst-case attack scenarios imaginable. Prudence requires that the United States consider the possibility of such attacks and plan responses accordingly. However, the best defense against nuclear and radiological terrorism is keeping fissile and radioactive materials out of the hands of terrorists. As Allison puts it:

> Is it conceivable that we would secure [all the fissile] material that could make possible nuclear terrorism? . . . Well, why not? The technologies for locking up things that are super dangerous or super valuable are pretty well developed. This is quite feasible if we said this is priority one, two, and three.[65]

Chapter Four

Chemical and Biological Attacks

Like nuclear and radiological attacks, the risk of a major chemical or biological terrorist attack is very low compared to the likelihood of a conventional attack. As Frank Cilluffo, a terrorism expert at the Center for Strategic and International Studies puts it: "Bugs . . . and gas are never going to take the place of bullets and bombs as the terrorist weapons of choice."[66] The technical difficulties involved in producing and using chemical and biological weapons are significant. Most of the deadliest chemicals and microorganisms—such as anthrax spores, the smallpox virus, and the Ebola virus—are very difficult to acquire. More importantly many chemicals and microorganisms are difficult to "weaponize." They are too delicate to be scattered via explosives, and to be effective they must be dispersed in aerosol form.

The difficulty of using even the most deadly chemical weapons was demonstrated in 1995 when Aum Shinrikyo, a Japanese cult, released deadly sarin gas into a crowded subway. The Council on Foreign Relations notes that the cult "spent an estimated $30 million on chemical weapons research and had many scientists in its ranks, but it managed to kill only 19 people with the nerve agent sarin—both because it encountered problems making sarin, experts say, and because it had difficulty using it as a mass-casualty weapon."[67]

Nevertheless the potential consequences of a successful chemical or biological attack are so daunting that preparing for and responding to such attacks has become a major focus of homeland security efforts. An effective response can significantly reduce casualties. The worst consequences of a chemical or biological attack may be averted if first responders and the public health community are adequately prepared.

Military Chemical Weapons

Among the different types of WMD, chemical weapons are the least high tech—they require less technological expertise to develop than do nuclear or biological weapons—and therefore thought to be a likely choice for terrorists. Chemical

Training emergency personnel to respond to chemical and biological attacks has become a security priority all over the world. Here, an Australian firefighter practices decontaminating a victim.

agents are also more readily available than biological agents. Chemical weapons basically work by dispersing poison (usually in gaseous form) into a small area.

The deadliest chemical weapons use nerve agents, which are capable of disrupting the human nervous system and paralyzing victims. Such agents do not occur in nature. They were first produced by German scientists seeking stronger pesticides in the 1930s and were later produced and stockpiled by the United States and the Soviet Union. Iraq used nerve agents in the 1980–1988 Iran-Iraq war, and the United States also suspects Syria, Egypt, Iran, Libya, and North Korea of harboring nerve gas stockpiles. Nerve gases are all colorless, odorless, tasteless liquids that vaporize into gaseous form. The two most well-known nerve gases are sarin and VX.

Sarin paralyzes the muscles of its victims and causes death by suffocation. About one liquid drop is enough to kill a person in a few minutes, but sarin dissipates very quickly in gaseous form. If administered promptly the drugs atropine and oxime can serve as an antidote to sarin. Military troops

In 1992 an Israeli plane carrying sarin nerve gas crashed into this Amsterdam apartment building. In the hands of terrorists, chemicals like sarin gas can become dangerous weapons.

who may face chemical warfare carry autoinjectors (syringes that inject automatically at the press of a button) of these drugs, and some cities, such as Hartford, Connecticut, and Boston, piloted projects to provide police, firefighters, and emergency personnel with nerve-agent antidote kits.

VX is the deadliest nerve agent ever created. Even small amounts absorbed through the skin can kill within minutes. The antidote for VX is similar to sarin's, but because VX acts so quickly, the antidote would need to be administered almost immediately. Both VX and sarin are difficult to produce and are believed to be beyond the means of the al-Qaeda terrorist network. A greater danger is that terrorist groups may be able to steal or purchase nerve agents from a nation's military stockpiles.

Another type of military chemical weapon that terrorists might seek to steal, purchase, or manufacture is mustard gas. First used in World War I, mustard gas is not a nerve agent and is not nearly as deadly as sarin or VX. However it is much more widely available in some Third World and eastern European countries, and it is much easier to produce than nerve agents. For these reasons some experts feel that it may be the chemical weapon of choice for terrorist groups.

Mustard gas is a blistering agent. It causes blistering of the skin, inflammation of the eyes or even blindness and, if inhaled, can cause damage to the lungs and other organs. Unlike nerve agents, exposure to mustard gas is disabling but not usually fatal, and the gas's effects are not felt immediately but instead take two to forty-eight hours to develop. There is no antidote for mustard gas. Instead treatment consists of decontaminating those exposed and using painkillers, antiburn powders, skin ointments, and other techniques to treat the injuries.

Household and Industrial Chemicals

While military-grade chemical agents make frightening chemical weapons, many homeland security officials are also concerned about more common chemicals that are widely available in the United States. As the National Research Council notes, the United States "stores, produces, and transports large quantities of toxic industrial agents. Certain of these (such as chlorine and phosgene) have actually been used as chemical weapons . . . others (volatile acids, certain industrial chemical intermediates) could cause numerous casualties if released in large quantities."[68] In fact some homeland security officials are more concerned about the threat from common chemicals than the threat of mustard gas or nerve agents. "I just believe that at the end of the day, it's a lot easier getting something that's available here in the United States than trying to sneak in sarin,"[69] says Jerry Hauer, acting assistant secretary for public health preparedness at the U.S. Department of Health and Human Services (HHS).

Chlorine and phosgene are both poisonous. The most plausible attack scenario involving these and other gases would be for terrorists to release them in an enclosed space where a large number of people gather, such as a subway station or an airport. Other concerns are that terrorists might attempt to poison food or water supplies (although the latter threat is considered unlikely, since the chemicals would be severely diluted and probably quickly discovered or neutralized through existing water treatment procedures). Terrorists could also disperse toxic agents or target large storehouses of toxic substances with conventional explosives in order to disperse hazardous substances into the environment. As journalist Guy F. Arnet writes: "Just as we could not believe that terrorists would fly airplanes into buildings, we cannot begin to think of all the ways terrorists might use chemical weapons."[70]

Because of the threat that hazardous chemicals pose, monitoring them has become a significant part of the overall U.S. homeland security strategy. Port and transportation authorities are monitoring chemical shipments more closely, and law enforcement agencies are working with the chemical industry to improve security at chemical facilities. At the

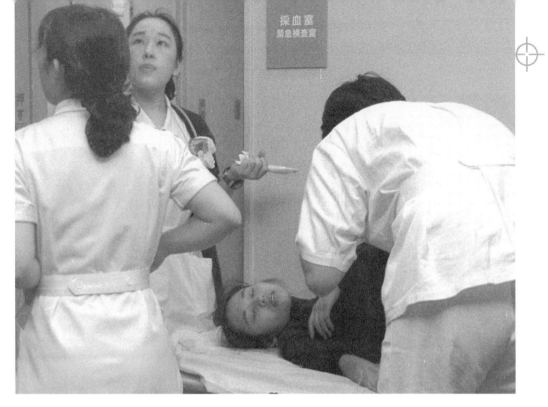

採血室
緊急検査室

same time local and federal government agencies are working to prepare for the consequences of a chemical attack.

Protecting Against a Chemical Attack

The main ways to protect against chemical attack are through physical protection, medicine and antidotes, and decontamination. Physical protection consists simply of not allowing a chemical agent to come in contact with one's body. On the most basic level, this consists of getting away from, and upwind of, the hazardous agent. Physical protection may also be achieved by what the DHS calls "shielding in place"—that is, finding an enclosed room that is sealed off from the outside air. The DHS has recommended that people keep duct tape and plastic sheeting in their homes in order to seal windows and ventilation ducts in the event of a chemical attack.

Physical protection is also achieved through the use of masks that prevent the inhalation of harmful gases. To this end a simple cloth mask provides little protection but is better than nothing. Air-purifying respirators—commonly

Doctors treat a patient exposed to sarin gas. Although chemicals like sarin pose a considerable threat, security officials are also concerned with the availability of common chemicals like chlorine.

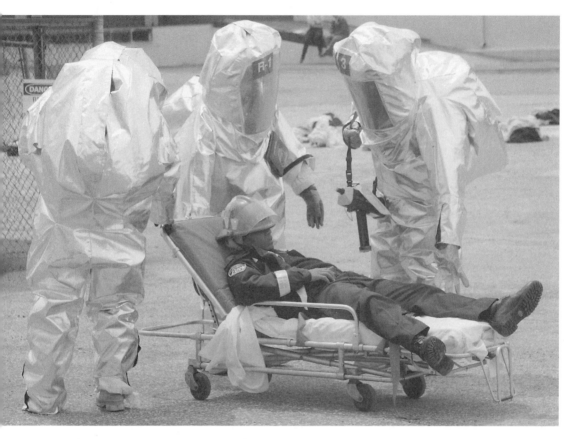

During a drill in New York, first responders rush a victim from the site of a simulated chemical attack. Moving upwind of a chemical agent helps protect people from exposure.

referred to simply as gas masks—provide a higher level of protection. Full-face gas masks also protect the eyes. These types of masks are likely to be used by first responders at the scene of a WMD attack.

The best respiratory protection, however, comes from a system in which the user is not inhaling outside air at all but is breathing safe, compressed air. The best system for this is a self-contained breathing apparatus (SCBA), in which a supply of air is stored in tanks on the user's back, much like the tanks used by scuba divers. In another system the user wears a supplied-air breathing apparatus (SABA), in which the user's mask is connected to a central air supply via a long hose called an umbilical line. Because hazardous agents can be absorbed through the skin, full physical protection also requires the use of a hazmat suit.

Hazmat Teams and Decontamination

In addition to police, firefighters, and emergency medical personnel, first responders to chemical and biological attacks will also involve another group—the hazmat team. Over six hundred local and state hazmat teams—groups of hazardous-materials specialists—exist in the United States. Hazmat teams are part of any city's or state's emergency-response operations, and they deal with all types of chemical spills, injuries, and accidents. In some areas the hazmat team is part of the fire company, and many firefighters and emergency medical personnel are trained to respond to hazmat incidents. Carl Reynolds, director of the chemical industry's Chemical Transportation Center, says that America's hazmat teams "get about 150 calls a day [nationwide], all the way from a pint paint can [spill] to a major accident."[71]

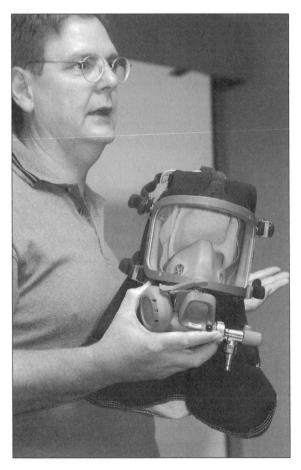

A self-contained breathing apparatus like this one protects people from inhaling air contaminated by chemicals.

The first task for hazmat units is to identify the harmful agent and begin providing decontamination, antidotes, and medication to victims. Antidotes and medical treatment are of little use if the harmful agent is still on the victim's person. Therefore rapid decontamination is a priority. In simple terms decontamination consists of stripping the victim of contaminated clothing and rinsing the person down with water or more specialized cleansing agents. At the scene of a WMD attack, first responders would likely set up "decon stations" for this process. All victims would need to pass through these stations before leaving the scene of the attack, since one of the greatest dangers of a WMD attack is that victims fleeing the scene could spread hazardous substances to others.

Biological Toxins

Many of the steps involved in responding to a chemical attack apply to a biological attack as well. Physical protection from the biological agent in question—via shielding in an isolated room or through gas masks and hazmat suits—would likely be the safest course of action for those in the vicinity of the attack. Hazmat teams would be called in, and decontamination would be a priority.

In fact some of the biological agents that terrorists might use as weapons act very much like chemical weapons. Ricin, a toxin that occurs naturally in the husks of castor beans (that are processed to produce castor oil) is such an agent. Because it is naturally occurring, ricin is classified as a biological rather than a chemical agent. Because castor beans are common throughout the world, it would be fairly easy for terrorists to obtain ricin. In fact ricin was found in the caves in Afghanistan in November 2001 during the search for al-Qaeda, and British antiterror squads seized a small batch in London in January 2003. From an attack-response perspective, ricin is much like a chemical weapon. The agent could be dispersed in powder or liquid form, and one milligram of ricin is enough to kill an adult. Exposure causes flulike symptoms, there is no antidote (although researchers are working on one), and death occurs within three to four days.

Another biological agent with properties akin to chemical weapons is botulinum toxin, a deadly substance produced by the bacterium *Clostridium botulinum.* It is sometimes found in undercooked or improperly canned food. Botulinum toxin is the strongest toxin known, being 1 million times stronger than sarin nerve gas. Iran, Iraq, North Korea, and Syria have developed, or are believed to be developing, botulinum toxin as a weapon, presumably to be dispersed in aerosol form. Like chemical nerve agents, botulinum toxin causes muscle paralysis and respiratory failure. It is much slower acting than nerve agents, with symptoms appearing within two to three days of exposure. If diagnosed early, victims can be treated with an antitoxin, and supportive care, which may include ventilators (breathing machines), which can sustain the patient for weeks or months while the paralysis slowly improves.

Anthrax

While ricin is poisonous and botulinum toxin causes paralysis, the threat more often associated with biological weapons is infectious disease—disease caused by the growth of viruses, bacteria, or other microorganisms. Anthrax, an infectious disease caused by the spore-forming bacterium *Bacillus anthracis*, may be contracted through the skin via cuts or abrasion, through the respiratory system via inhalation, or through the intestinal tract via ingestion of contaminated food. Depending on the path of infection, within a few days victims may experience skin bumps and ulcers, breathing problems, or vomiting and abdominal pain. Inhalation anthrax is the most deadly form of the disease. Treatment with antibiotics is usually not effective once symptoms begin (although antibiotics can be effective if the disease is caught early).

Anthrax became one of the threats most associated with bioterror in the fall of 2001 after four letters—including ones addressed to Senators Tom Daschle and Patrick Leahy, and news anchor Tom Brokaw—were found to be contaminated with anthrax spores. Twenty-three people, including eleven postal workers and eight employees of media organizations where some letters were received, contracted anthrax, and five of them died as a result.

Experts also worry that terrorists might try to disperse anthrax in more dangerous ways. Rick Weiss of the *Washington Post* reports that: "A little more than two pounds of anthrax spores spilled into the air over a city the size of New York could be expected to kill more than one hundred

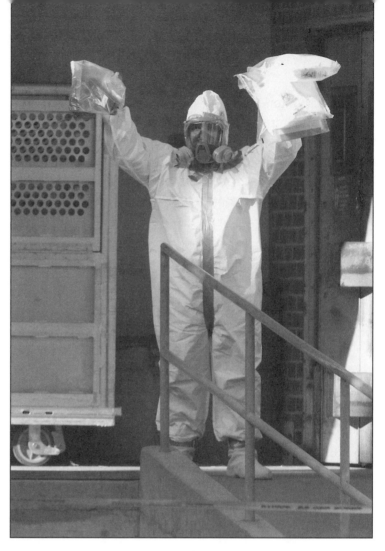

An investigator holds up samples taken during an inspection of a New Jersey post office for anthrax contamination. Spreading anthrax is one of the most deadly forms of bioterrorism.

and twenty thousand people,"[72] according to computer models of terrorist acts. A vaccine exists for anthrax, but it has only been produced in limited quantities and, in order to be effective, it must be administered six times over the course of eighteen months. The U.S. military, however, does vaccinate troops that spend more than two weeks a year in high-risk areas such as the Persian Gulf.

The Threat of Contagion: Smallpox and Other Bioweapons

Although anthrax is a deadly disease, it is not contagious. It is extremely unlikely that anthrax would be transmitted from one person to another via bodily contact or a sneeze. In contrast most other bioterror threats are so menacing because they can spread from person to person. In fact the major threat of bioterrorism—what makes a biological attack different from other WMD threats—is the potential for biological agents to start an epidemic. A terrorist attack with a contagious biological agent could trigger a disease outbreak that would increase the number of casualties exponentially. Furthermore a biological attack using these agents may not be immediately obvious, since it would take days for people to become sick, during which time they might be exposing others to the agent.

Among the contagious biological threats, smallpox has received the most attention from both the media and from homeland security officials, and for good reason. As U.S. Army physician Kevin Coonan puts it: "Few diseases have rivaled smallpox as a cause of human suffering and death."[73] Smallpox is extremely contagious, and like the common cold can be transmitted from person to person through the air or through contaminated clothing or surfaces. The virus causes flulike symptoms to appear within one to two weeks of infection, and then victims develop pus-filled lesions (similar to chicken-pox sores) on the face, arms, and legs. Antibiotics are not very effective in treating smallpox, and the disease is lethal in about 30 percent of cases.

Smallpox was one of the most devastating diseases until vaccination became widespread in the twentieth century. In 1979 the World Health Organization officially declared that smallpox had been eradicated through a massive, worldwide vaccination program. The United States abandoned routine smallpox vaccination in 1972 and, worldwide, no one has contracted the disease since 1978. The only known remaining strains of the virus are stored in high-security research facilities in the United States and Moscow. However, homeland security officials are concerned that other samples of the smallpox virus could still exist. The chance that terrorists could gain access to a sample of smallpox virus is remote, but if they did, the millions of Americans born since 1972 would be completely susceptible to infection. Terrorist use of smallpox is, like the use of WMD a low-probability, high-consequence threat.

In addition to smallpox the Centers for Disease Control and Prevention (CDC) has listed bubonic plague, tularemia, and hemorrhagic fevers as possible bioterror threats. Bubonic plague is the highly contagious disease that killed one-third of the population of Europe in the fourteenth century. Modern sanitation and public health practices have largely eliminated the conditions that allow *Yersinia pestis*, the bacterium that causes the plague, to thrive, but experts worry that terrorists might try to disperse the bacterium in aerosol form. Bioterrorism experts also fear that terrorists might try to weaponize pneumonic plague, a rarer, more lethal form of the disease. There is no vaccine for pneumonic plague, but if administered quickly, antibiotics can effectively fight both forms of the disease. Tularemia, a plague-like disease also known as rabbit fever, can also be treated with antibiotics.

Vaccination

As with WMD threats in general, the response to a biological attack would depend on the specific agent used in the attack. For those agents for which a vaccine exists—notably smallpox—emergency vaccination is certainly a major part of the response strategy.

The United States has over 200 million doses of smallpox vaccination, enough for every American. However, smallpox vaccination has risks. Historically between fourteen and fifty-two of every 1 million people who received the vaccine experienced life-threatening reactions, and one or two of every 1 million died. In December 2002 President Bush announced plans to vaccinate five hundred thousand health care workers, but the plan met with resistance, largely from the health care workers themselves. However, in the

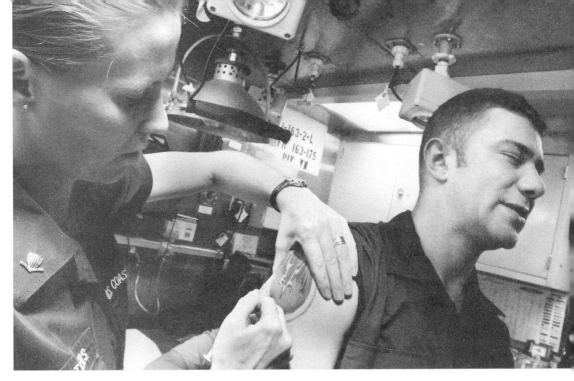

case of smallpox, vaccination even three days after exposure to the smallpox virus is usually effective in stopping the disease.

A member of the U.S. Coast Guard winces at his anthrax vaccine. The U.S. government has prepared for biological attack by stockpiling reserves of anthrax and smallpox vaccines.

Doctors, nurses, and emergency workers would still be the first to be vaccinated in the event of a smallpox or similar biological attack so that they can, in turn, vaccinate others. One strategy used in preventative vaccination is known as ring vaccination, in which contaminated individuals are identified and the people connected to them are vaccinated in an expanding circle. Federal officials announced in September 2002 that, ultimately, the discovery of even a single case of smallpox will lead to voluntary vaccinations nationwide. While vaccinations are being administered, individuals known to be infected would likely be quarantined.

Quarantines

Quarantines are isolation measures imposed to prevent the spread of disease. In the strictest form of quarantine, a certain area—which could range anywhere from a single building to an entire metropolitan area—is declared an infection risk, and no one is allowed into or out of that area.

Many homeland security planners are reluctant to make rigid quarantines a part of their emergency-response procedures because individuals in a possibly infectious area are likely to resist the quarantine. Abraham McLaughlin and Michelle Dent of the *Christian Science Monitor* report that: "Quarantine history includes serious violence. In Muncie, Indiana, in 1893, residents resisted a smallpox-induced quarantine. Violence broke out, and several officials were shot."[74] Strict quarantines must be enforced to be effective, and that raises the possibility of grim scenarios that few emergency-response planners want to contemplate. For example Randall Larsen of Analytical Services Inc., known as the ANSER Institute for Homeland Security, says that with quarantines, "you have to decide whether you're going to shoot grandma in her pickup [truck] who's trying to leave the city."[75]

There are potentially effective, less extreme quarantine actions that could be implemented in response to a biological attack. A FEMA document explains that quarantine can involve "closing of public transportation, limiting public gatherings, and limiting intercity travel."[76] Many of these protective actions are designed to limit people's contact with one another (in order to curb the spread of contagion) without resorting to a strict quarantine. Such measures were largely successful in containing the Spring 2003 outbreaks of Severe Acute Respiratory Syndrome (SARS) in China and Canada.

Strengthening the Public Health System

While the response to any type of terrorist attack will rely heavily on emergency medical personnel, an effective response to a chemical or biological attack will depend on the quality of America's public health system. In the case of a biological attack, health workers may even take the place of police and firefighters as the very first responders.

Unlike most other conceivable terrorist attacks, a biological attack might not be immediately noticeable. If agents such as the smallpox virus or anthrax spores were released discreetly, it would take days or weeks for anyone to develop symptoms. "The first sign of [a silent] attack," as bioterror researcher Rebecca Katz explains, "is likely to be the seemingly innocent event of a small number of people going to their private doctors' office or the emergency rooms of their local hospitals, complaining of flu-like symptoms."[77] Once such a phenomenon is identified, medical laboratories will work to determine if a biological attack has taken place. The effectiveness of the public health system in this process is critical. The longer the attack discovery process takes, the more people will become sick or die.

To adequately respond to attack, says Katz, the nation needs "a strong infectious-disease surveillance system, vaccine development and pharmaceutical stockpiles, scientific research, communications networks, laboratory capacity,

In the case of a biological attack, health workers, like these two Pennsylvania nurses, may become first responders.

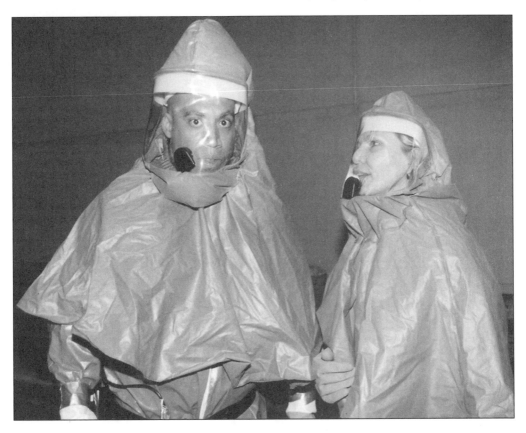

hospital readiness, and professional training."[78]Many communities lack such strong public health resources, however. The Bush administration's *National Strategy for Homeland Security* acknowledged that: "A major act of biological terrorism would almost certainly overwhelm existing state, local, and privately owned health care capabilities."[79]

Despite their limited resources, hospitals across the country are doing what they can to prepare for bioterrorism. They are beefing up supplies of necessary vaccines and antibiotics, training doctors and nurses to identify and treat the major biological threats, and developing bioterror-response plans. Ultimately, however, more funding for local hospitals and other public health facilities is needed to improve America's biological and chemical attack-response capabilities. The federal government earmarked billions of dollars for hospital preparedness, bioterrorism research, and new disease-surveillance and attack-response systems, but it will take a long time for changes to be implemented.

State and Federal Efforts

In the meantime state and federal resources are in place to help local first responders in the event of a WMD attack. For example the CDC initiated the National Pharmaceutical Stockpile (NPS) Program in 1999. The NPS is comprised of pharmaceuticals, vaccines, medical supplies, and medical equipment that might be difficult for local hospitals to obtain in the event of a major emergency. The program is capable of delivering, according to the CDC, "a complete package of medical material—to include nearly everything a state will need to respond to a broad range of threats,"[80] along with a small team to assist in distribution of the materials anywhere in the nation within twelve hours.

The CDC also put together an Epidemic Intelligence Service of almost 150 professional field epidemiologists trained in detecting and investigating infectious disease outbreaks. Similarly the DHS initiated a plan to organize smallpox

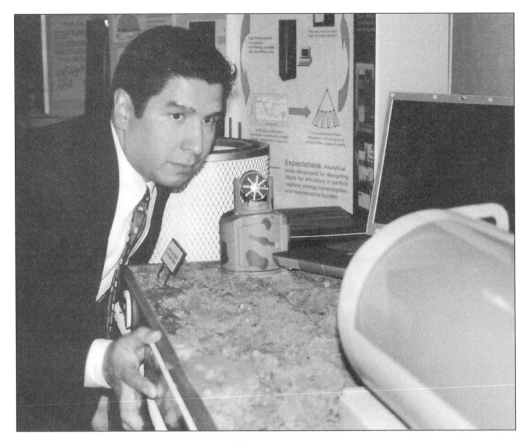

response teams in each state to investigate and evaluate initial suspected cases of smallpox and initiate measures to control the outbreak.

These programs are just a few of the many attack-response and preparedness efforts managed by the federal government. The critical first response to any terrorist attack is fundamentally a local effort. But in the event of a chemical, biological, or even nuclear attack, an effective response must also involve state and federal agencies.

A military scientist poses with a chemical and biological detection system. Such devices help medical personnel to detect and investigate chemical contamination and outbreaks of disease.

Chapter Five

Challenges and Issues

H omeland security is a sensitive issue. Just about every decision made about homeland security—from a small town's debate over whether or not to increase the local fire station's budget to the federal government's creation of the DHS—has its critics. In general the scrutiny under which homeland security policies are developed is a good thing. As flaws and weaknesses in current policies are exposed, better policies are developed. However some of the fundamental questions surrounding America's ability to respond to terrorism are so controversial that they may never be resolved. Awareness of these issues is vital to understanding the challenges facing homeland security officials.

Government Secrecy

For example one of the key tenets of homeland security strategy is to keep terrorists guessing about the specifics of security measures. Whether it is detailed information such as building plans and guard schedules, or general information such as which potential targets the government is trying hardest to protect, the sentiment among homeland security planners is that the less information terrorists have the better.

One controversial aspect of this mindset is a growing aura of government secrecy in regard to homeland security issues. Many of the specifics about U.S. vulnerabilities and the security measures designed to protect them are being kept secret from the general U.S. public. Laura Parker et al., in *USA Today*, report that since the September 11 attacks: "Hundreds of thousands of public documents have been removed from government Web sites. Other public information has been edited, and access to some materials has been made more difficult."[81] These documents include maps and descriptions of security procedures at power plants, dams, gas and oil pipelines, chemical storage sites, government buildings, and national monuments. Homeland security officials argue that such information would obviously be of use to terrorists.

But both the federal and state governments have also been hesitant to divulge the specifics of many attack-preparedness efforts and emergency-response plans, information that many people think should be available to concerned citizens. Since the 2001 terrorist attacks, at least forty states have proposed changes to their open records laws to keep evacuation routes, emergency-response plans, and emergency health procedures secret. "We seem to be shifting to the public's need to know instead of the public's right to know,"[82] says Gary Boss, director of a government watchdog group.

Members of Connecticut's Homeland Security team arrive at a meeting to discuss ways to strengthen the state's security operations.

Beyond concerns about open government and the public's right to know, many critics feel that government secrecy may undermine the public's confidence in homeland security efforts. This was evident in many people's criticism of the DHS's Homeland Security Advisory System. Although the DHS moved the nation to orange alert—indicating a high risk of terrorist attack—several times following September 11, little information was divulged regarding the reasons for the increased alert or what specific steps the federal government takes at this increased alert level. "The public isn't served if the government issues terrorism alerts without telling Americans what to do," write the editors of *USA Today.* "That doesn't empower Americans. It scares them."[83] The government must therefore strike a difficult balance between keeping the public informed on the one hand and not inadvertently benefiting terrorists on the other.

A (Largely) Civilian Framework

Another area in which the government must strike a balance is in how involved the military is in homeland security efforts. The military's role in homeland security is a complex issue. Historically the military has been reluctant to involve itself in the nation's domestic affairs because it takes away from their international duties. For example Captain Aaron Weiss of the U.S. Marine Corps writes that: "Preoccupation with . . . peacetime duties," including homeland security measures, "will leave the active-duty military unfit to engage a real military opponent."[84] Furthermore the United States has traditionally maintained a clear separation between military and civilian authority, in order to help prevent political leaders from using military force to impose their will, as tyrants have done throughout history. The Posse Comitatus Act, passed by Congress in 1878, prohibits the military from engaging in domestic law-enforcement activities or security operations, except in certain situations such as when the president declares a national emergency.

Involving the military in homeland security efforts is, therefore, a controversial issue. In fact the term homeland security came into widespread use in part because of this controversy, evolving largely as a counterpart to the term national security. Homeland security—gathering intelligence on terrorist threats and preparing for and responding to terrorist attacks on U.S. soil—is a largely nonmilitary effort. National security—dealing with threats posed by other countries—is the military's realm. However the distinction between homeland security and national security is far from absolute. The two concepts often overlap, and there are at least two areas in which the military is an active part of America's attack-response framework.

The first is the National Guard, a component of the U.S. military that has traditionally served in a civilian support role. The Army National Guard and Air National Guard are composed of part-time soldiers, more than sixty thousand of whom are on active duty in homeland security operations. "The Army National Guard," writes policy analyst Jack Spencer, "maintains over 3,000 armories around the country, while the Air National Guard has 140 units throughout the United States and its territories."[85] Since September 11 the Air National Guard flies combat air patrols twenty-four hours a day searching for stray aircraft—if they find any, they have the authority to escort it to a landing strip, or if necessary, shoot it down.

Tom Ridge (right) converses with U.S. Customs agents. As Director of Homeland Security, Ridge has the difficult task of coordinating the efforts of many federal agencies.

"If a situation similar to September 11 repeated itself," write guardsmen Jon Power's and Robert Stephenson, "the pilots would be in a position to prevent another act of terrorism."[86] Immediately after September 11, the National Guard was assigned to augment police efforts in New York City as well as to aid U.S. customs officials at the borders linking the United States to Canada and Mexico. They were also assigned to guard the nation's ports, bridges, and nuclear power plants in response to elevated DHS alert levels. The National Guard could also be called on to support local response efforts in the event of terrorist attacks.

The other major area in which the military is involved with homeland security efforts is in dealing with WMD. Protecting against chemical and biological weapons was a priority for the military long before it became a major homeland security concern. The Defense Threat Reduction Agency (DTRA) is the agency within the Department of Defense responsible for developing solutions to counter WMD threats. Much of the research conducted by the DTRA benefits both military and homeland security operations.

Limiting the military's homeland security operations to the National Guard and DTRA research helps to prevent the United States from becoming a police state in which liberty is sacrificed for security. Americans want to be secure from terrorism without feeling stifled by security measures. America's leaders must balance the need for government secrecy and an increased military presence in everyday life with the need to maintain an open, democratic society that Americans cherish.

Difficult as this may be, the nation faces even greater challenges in implementing some of its most basic homeland security goals such as providing better training and equipment to first responders. The problem, in a word, is money.

Funding First Responders

"America's first line of defense in the aftermath of any terrorist attack is its first responder community—police officers, firefighters, emergency medical providers, public works personnel, and emergency management officials," states President Bush's *National Strategy for Homeland Security.* "Nearly three million state and local first responders regularly put their lives on the line to save the lives of others and make our country safer."[87]

However, in order to respond effectively to WMD attacks, emergency workers need specialized training and equipment that most cities do not have the means to provide. For example, as Ratnesar, in a *Time* magazine report puts it: "Hospitals say they can't train enough employees to effectively spot and treat victims of biological attacks; fire departments can't afford to buy the haz-mat suits needed to guard against deadly germs."[88]

Lack of funding is a major problem. While hundreds of millions of dollars in security funding was provided to state and city governments, legislation to provide billions more stalled in Congress due to concerns about the federal budget and the nation's ailing economy. Baltimore mayor, Martin

In this 2002 speech at the base of Mount Rushmore, President Bush criticizes the Senate for not allocating more funding to homeland security.

O'Malley, voices a common view that America's cities need more help from the federal government: "You cannot fund an adequate level of homeland security on local property taxes and the proceeds of firehouse bingo."[89] O'Malley expresses a common opinion that funding homeland defense is a federal, rather than a local or state, responsibility.

While there are many local leaders calling for more funding for first responders, there are also critics on the other side of the issue who worry that the United States may be spending too much on homeland security efforts. Their question How much spending is enough? is a difficult one to answer. "We can spend ourselves into bankruptcy," says Randy Larsen of the ANSER Institute for Homeland Security. "We just can't defend ourselves against every attack."[90] Again the challenge facing America's leaders is to strike a balance—in this case between adequately funding homeland security efforts while ensuring that concerns about terrorism do not put undue strain on the economy.

Beyond First Responders

The challenge of managing homeland security efforts becomes more evident when one moves beyond first responders to the broader mosaic of state and federal agencies responsible for homeland security. As the *National Strategy for Homeland Security* puts it, homeland security "is an exceedingly complex mission that requires coordinated and focused effort from our entire society—the federal government, state and local governments, the private sector, and the American people. . . . A national strategy requires a national effort."[91] A nationwide effort is more crucial to America's attack-preparedness and emergency-response efforts than any other aspect of homeland security (such as intelligence gathering or border control).

Serving as a bridge between local first responders and higher levels of services are the nation's city and state offices of emergency management (OEMs), which provide the leadership needed to coordinate first responders' efforts. At the federal level the Office of Domestic Preparedness (ODP), part of the DHS, works with city and state OEMs to enhance the abilities of first responders by providing terrorism-response training and technical assistance.

In addition to providing management and leadership, state and federal agencies work with first responders in the event of an attack, serving as the backup and support to the responders on the front lines. For example, one of the most difficult problems that local and state governments are likely to face in responding to a terrorist attack—especially one involving WMD—is a shortage of medical facilities, supplies, and personnel in the face of large numbers of attack victims. Several agencies and programs exist specifically to supplement a community's resources in the event of such a disaster.

The American Red Cross, though not part of the government, works closely with local governments during times

Tom Ridge applauds President Bush. Ridge works closely with the president, Congress, and state and local government officials to improve America's ability to effectively respond to terrorist attack.

of major crises. The Red Cross would be a major part of medical-relief efforts in the wake of a major terrorist incident, supplementing the efforts of local public health authorities with emergency medical treatment and supplies. Beyond emergency medical relief, the Red Cross also provides food, shelter, and mental health services to disaster victims.

The Department of Health and Human Services (HHS) also aids in medical-relief efforts, primarily its OEM. Under the OEM's National Disaster Medical System (NDMS), the federal government can dispatch groups of medical personnel designed to provide emergency medical care during a disaster or other emergency. Since terrorists are more likely to target large cities, the HHS may employ its Metropolitan Medical Response System (MMRS) instead of, or in addition to, the NDMS. The purpose of both NDMS and MMRS teams is to support local public health efforts, but MMRS teams receive more specialized training in dealing with WMD attacks. In fact the MMRS system includes four geographically dispersed teams officially known as the National Medical Response Teams for Weapons of Mass Destruction.

Coordinating It All

Responsibilities for homeland security are dispersed among more than 100 different government organizations, dozens of which would play significant roles in responding to a terrorist attack. In the aftermath of September 11, the government was widely criticized for the complicated, seemingly haphazard array of agencies and programs charged with protecting America from terrorism. The DHS was created, in part, to help coordinate the diverse array of local, state, and federal programs that make up America's emergency-response system. This part of the DHS's mission is certainly an ongoing effort. The DHS, Congress, the president, and state and local government officials are constantly working to improve the government's terrorism-response efforts, and new homeland security initiatives regularly make news headlines.

The DHS incorporates twenty-two other federal agencies, including the Immigration and Naturalization Service, the U.S. Coast Guard, and the U.S. Border Patrol that operated more or less independently of one another prior to September 11. Because the DHS is a cabinet-level agency, the White House is able to work directly with it to manage homeland security efforts. The creation of the DHS has greatly helped to reduce—though not completely eliminate—the bureaucracy, redundancy, and confusion that sometimes characterized U.S. counterterrorism efforts prior to September 11.

For example, before the creation of the DHS, FEMA was the principal federal agency responsible for disaster response and assistance. FEMA's disaster-response capabilities have included attack-response duties for decades. According to one official who had a hand in creating the DHS:

> Under the Reagan administration, unseen by the public, FEMA had a strong national-security capability for preparedness to deal with the consequences of a war at home. All of that was lost when the Soviet Union came apart, and that side of FEMA was simply abolished. Now we're back to needing this kind of capability, and putting FEMA in a new department offers the opportunity to get there.[92]

FEMA's attack-response responsibilities overlapped with those of several other agencies. For example the FBI's National Infrastructure Protection Center (NIPC) and National Office of Domestic Preparedness (NODP) also shared responsibility for responding to terrorist attacks but had no direct connection to FEMA.

Instead of operating behind the scenes, as it did during the Cold War, FEMA is now part of the DHS and has a major role within that evolving department. The DHS is comprised of five main divisions, or directorates—Border and Transportation Security, Emergency Preparedness and Response, Science and Technology, Information Analysis and Infrastructure Protection, and Management. The DHS's Emergency Preparedness and Response Directorate is the

Immigrants line up outside the Immigration and Naturalization Service, one of twenty-two federal agencies managed by the DHS.

one charged with attack-response efforts, and FEMA is the primary agency within this directorate, with agencies such as NIPC and NODP under its lead. FEMA's mission continues to be to prepare for, prevent, respond to, and facilitate recovery from disasters. As such FEMA would play a major role in coordinating the efforts of all federal agencies and programs in the event of a terrorist attack.

Achieving a Unified Response

While the DHS has achieved some success in making sure that federal agencies coordinate their efforts, it still faces the challenge of getting state and local governments to follow the federal government's lead. As DHS director, Tom Ridge, admits: "The federal government has no first responders."[93] It must therefore rely on state and city governments that often choose not to comply with DHS requests. For example, in spring 2003, the DHS announced that the nation was at orange alert due to increased risk of terrorist attack, and Ridge called on many state governors to deploy the National Guard to protect bridges and railroads. But most governors refused because they felt there was no specific threat to their states.

The DHS must deal with the mayors of America's major cities as well. In April 2003, again citing the possibility of terrorist retaliation for the invasion of Iraq, Ridge asked Philadelphia mayor, John Street, to close a road near Independence Hall where the Liberty Bell is kept. Street refused, citing tourism and traffic concerns.

Thus one of the biggest challenges facing the DHS, as journalist Alex Fryer explains, is "ironing out the role of federal government and how it relates to the cities and states that carry out the war on terrorism."[94] The federal government does not have the constitutional authority to assume control over a local police station, firehouse, or hospital. If there is a disagreement between federal and local officials, says Ridge, "then it's my job to communicate personally with whoever is objecting and figure out a way to make them do it otherwise."[95]

The challenge the DHS faces in working with state and federal governments is part of the broader trend in which

Coast Guard marshals provide security for a passenger ship. Homeland security concerns here forced agencies from different levels of government to work closely together.

PROTECTING
THE
HOMELAND

President Bush poses with DHS members. President Bush continues to work with the Department of Homeland Security in an ongoing effort to create a unified homeland security response.

homeland security concerns are forcing different levels of government to work more closely together than ever before. Although homeland security is a national issue, attack preparedness is very much a local concern. As Seattle mayor, Greg Nickels, puts it: "When a disaster occurs, people do not call the White House. They call 911."[96]

Achieving a unified homeland security response, coordinating the various federal agencies responsible for homeland security, and managing the controversial issues of government secrecy and military involvement in homeland security are all ongoing efforts. These issues will never be fully resolved to everyone's satisfaction, just as the American homeland will never be completely secure. Nevertheless U.S. leaders continue to seek the best possible solutions to these difficult issues, just as they strive to maintain security in the face of unpredictable terrorist threats.

Notes

Introduction: America the Vigilant

1. President George W. Bush, "State of the Union," White House, January 29, 2002. www.whitehouse.gov.

2. Quoted in *Human Events*, "Forewarned, But Not Forestalled?" May 27, 2002, p. 7.

3. Quoted in *Human Events*, "Forewarned."

4. Quoted in Liz Marlantes and Abraham McLaughlin, "Gauging the Seriousness of New Terror Warnings," *Christian Science Monitor*, May 23, 2002.

5. Freedberg, Sydney J. Jr., "Beyond the Blue Canaries,"*National Journal*, March 1, 2003, p. 638.

6. Council on Foreign Relations Task Force, "America—Still Unprepared, Still in Danger," Council on Foreign Relations, 2002. www.cfr.org.

7. Quoted in Romesh Ratnesar, "The State of Our Defense," *Time*, February 24, 2003, p. 24.

8. Quoted in Thomas Omestad, "Are We Safer?" *U.S. News & World Report*, September 2002, p. 61.

9. Ron Scherer, "A Homeland Reader for 'High' Alert," *Christian Science Monitor*, March 20, 2003, p. 1c.

10. Ratnesar, "The State of Our Defense," p. 24.

Chapter 1: Protecting and Preparing

11. Quoted in Alexandra Marks, "Flying the Fortified Skies," *Christian Science Monitor*, April 25, 2003, p. 3.

12. White House Office of Homeland Security, *National Strategy for Homeland Security*, July 2002. www.whitehouse.gov.

13. Quoted in White House Office of Homeland Security, *National Strategy for Homeland Security*, p. 20.

14. Brian Michael Jenkins, *Terrorism: Current and Long Term Threats*, testimony before the Senate Armed Services Subcommittee on Emerging Threats, November 15, 2001. www.rand.org.

15. Omestad, "Are We Safer?" p. 61.

16. Quoted in Chitra Ragavan et al., "Alert—and Anxious," *U.S. News & World Report*, March 31, 2001, p. 36.

17. Quoted in Siobhan Gorman and Sydney J. Freedberg Jr., "A Burnt-Orange Nation," *National Journal*, March 1, 2003, p. 638.

18. Quoted in Gorman and Freedberg, "A Burnt-Orange Nation."

19. Quoted in Spenser Hsu, "Worst-Case Scenario: Code Red Means It's Time to Put Plans into Action," *Washington Post*, March 16, 2003, p. A32.

20. Hsu, "Worst-Case Scenario," p. A32.

21. Quoted in *FEMA News*, "Homeland Security Helps Train Citizens for Emergencies with $19 Million for Community Emergency Response Teams," May 29, 2003. www.fema. gov.

22. Executive Session on Domestic Preparedness, *Beyond the Beltway: Focusing on Hometown Security.* John F. Kennedy School of Government, Harvard University, September 2002. http://bcsia.ksg.harvard.edu.

23. Quoted in Johnna A. Pro, "Homeland Security Affecting Emphasis of Local Fire Stations," *Pittsburgh Post-Gazette*, May 25, 2003, p. A1.

24. Quoted in Beverly Lumpkin, "Terror Test," *abcNEWS.com*, May 12, 2003. http://more.abcnews.go.com.

Chapter 2: The Basics of Emergency Response

25. Quoted in Ruth David, "Homeland Security: Building a National Strategy," *The Bridge*, Spring 2002, p. 28.

26. Executive Session on Domestic Preparedness, *Beyond the Beltway.*

27. Federal Emergency Management Agency, *Managing the Emergency Consequences of Terrorist Incidents: Interim Planning Guide for State and Local Governments*, July 2002. www.fema.org.

28. Frances Edward-Winslow, "Telling It Like It Is: The Role of the Media in Terrorism Response and Recovery," *Perspectives on Preparedness*, August 2002, p. 1.

29. Randy Atkins, "The News Media Could Be Our Weakest Link," *Washington Post*, January 26, 2003, p. B3.

30. Rachel Smolkin, "Girding for Terror," *American Journalism Review*, April 2003, p. 28.

31. Viktor Mayer-Schönberger, "Emergency Communications: The Quest for Interoperability in the United States and Europe," BCSIA Discussion Paper 2002–7, ESDP Discussion Paper ESDP-2002–03, John F. Kennedy School of Government, Harvard University, March 2002. http://ksgnotes1.harvard.edu.

32. Mayer-Schönberger, "Emergency Communications."

33. Dale Craig, "Communicating in a Crisis," *Journal of Counterterrorism and Homeland Security International*, Fall 2003.

34. Quoted in Craig, "Communicating in a Crisis."

35. Craig, "Communicating in a Crisis."

36. Quoted in *UF News*, "University of Florida Surgeon Calls on Medical Personnel to Revamp Terrorist Plans," September 6, 2002. www.napa.ufl.edu.

37. Joseph A. Barbera et al., "Ambulances to Nowhere: America's Critical Shortfall in Medical Preparedness for Catastrophic Terrorism," BCSIA Discussion Paper 2001–15, ESDP Discussion Paper ESDP-2001-07, John F. Kennedy School of Government, Harvard University, October 2001. www.home landdefense.org.

38. Quoted in "University of Florida Surgeon Calls on Medical Personnel to Revamp Terrorist Plans."

39. Council on Foreign Relations, "Hospital Emergency Rooms," *Terrorism: Questions & Answers*. www.terrorismanswers. com.

40. Johanna Neuman, "Mass Evacuations Present Massive Problems," *Los Angeles Times*, May 11, 2003, p. A28.

41. American Red Cross, "Terrorism: Preparing for the Unexpected," October 2001. www.redcross.org.

42. Neuman, "Mass Evacuations Present Massive Problems."

43. Quoted in David Eberhart, "Fallout Shelters Fall Short in the U.S.," *NewsMax.com*, February 15, 2002. www.newsmax.com.

44. Neuman, "Mass Evacuations Present Massive Problems."

45. Emergency Survival Program, "Learn Light Search and Rescue," ESP FOCUS, August 2003. www.cert-la.com.

46. Federal Emergency Management Agency, "FEMA Task Force Tools and Equipment," *Urban Search and Rescue Response System*. www.fema.gov.

47. Quoted in Scherer, "A Homeland Reader for 'High' Alert."

48. Executive Session on Domestic Preparedness, *Beyond the Beltway*, p. 6.

Chapter 3: Nuclear and Radiological Attacks

49. Executive Session on Domestic Preparedness, "A New National Priority: Enhancing Public Health and Safety Through Domestic Preparedness," *Perspectives on Preparedness*, March 2001. http://bcsia.ksg.harvard.edu.

50. Quoted in Michelle Mittlestadt, "Bioterror Focus May Obscure Greater Risk," *Dallas Morning News*, October 30, 2001, p. 1A.

51. Executive Session on Domestic Preparedness, "A New National Priority."

52. Graham Allison and Andrei Kokoshin, "The New Containment: An Alliance Against Nuclear Terrorism," *National Interest*, Fall 2002.

53. Bob Port, "Nuclear Terrorism: A 'Near-Term' Threat," *New York Daily News*, September 8, 2002, p. A8.

54. Quoted in Port, "Nuclear Terrorism," p. A8.

55. Allison and Kokoshin, "The New Containment."

56. Bill Nichols, Mimi Hall, and Peter Eisner, "The Next Terror Threat— 'The Future Is Here, I'm Afraid,'" *USA Today*, June 11, 2002, p. 1A.

57. Quoted in Sarah Estabrooks, "Nuclear Terrorism," *Ploughshares Monitor*, December 2001, p. 4.

58. Quoted in Douglas Pasternak, "A Nuclear Nightmare," *U.S. News & World Report*, September 17, 2001, p. 44.

59. Quoted in Nichols, Hall, and Eisner, "The Next Terror Threat."

60. Henry Kelly, *Testimony on Terrorist Nuclear Threat*, testimony before the Senate Committee on Foreign Relations, March 6, 2002. www.fas.org.

61. Kelly, *Testimony on Terrorist Nuclear Threat*.

62. Quoted in John J. Stanton, "Is the U.S. Prepared for Nuclear Terrorism?" *Security Management*, March 2002, p. 46.

63. Department of Homeland Security, "National Security Emergencies," *Emergencies and Disasters: Planning and Prevention*. www.dhs.gov.

64. Department of Homeland Security, "National Security Emergencies."

65. Graham Allison, "Encounter: Graham Allison," *Boston Globe*, December 1, 2002, p. 3.

Chapter 4: Chemical and Biological Attacks

66. Quoted in Mittlestadt, "Bioterror Focus May Obscure Greater Risk."

67. Council on Foreign Relations, "Responding to Chemical Attacks," *Terrorism: Questions & Answers*. www.terrorismanswers.com.

68. National Research Council, *Making the Nation Safer: The Role of Science and Technology for Countering Terrorism*. Washington, DC: National Academies Press, 2002, p. 111.

69. Quoted in *Bioterrorism Week*, "Terror Threat Extends to Common Chemicals, Officials Warn," April 28, 2003, p. 14.

70. Guy F. Arnet, "What You Can Do to Protect Yourself Against Chemical, Biological, and Nuclear Terrorism," *Backwoods Home Magazine*, May/June 2003, p. 8.

71. Quoted in Freedberg and Gorman, "A Burnt-Orange Nation," p. 700.

72. Rick Weiss, "Anthrax Response Plans Inadequate, Study Warns," *Washington Post*, March 18, 2003, p. A23.

73. Kevin Coonan, "One Year Later: Emergency Department Response to Biological Terrorism Part II: Smallpox, Viral Hemorrhagic Fevers, Tularemia, and Botulinum Toxins," *Trauma Reports*, November/December 2002, p. 1.

74. Abraham McLaughlin and Michelle Dent, "Lesson for U.S. Cities from Antiterror Drills," *Christian Science Monitor*, May 15, 2003, p. 1.

75. Quoted in McLaughlin and Dent, "Lesson for U.S. Cities from Antiterror Drills."

76. Federal Emergency Management Agency, *Managing the Emergency Consequences of Terrorist Incidents*, p. 28.

77. Rebecca Katz, "Public Health Preparedness: The Best Defense Against Biological Weapons," *Provocations*, Summer 2002, p. 69.

78. Katz, "Public Health Preparedness."

79. White House Office of Homeland Security, *National Strategy for Homeland Security*.

80. Centers for Disease Control and Prevention, "National Pharmaceutical Stockpile," *Public Health Emergency Preparedness and Response*. www.bt.cdc.gov.

Chapter 5: Challenges and Issues

81. Laura Parker et al., "Secure Often Means Secret," *USA Today*, May 16, 2002, p. 1A.

82. Quoted in Parker et al., "Secure Often Means Secret," p. 1A.

83. *USA Today*, "Color-Coded Terror Alerts Too Difficult to Decipher," September 26, 2002, p. 10A.

84. Aaron Weiss, "When Terror Strikes, Who Should Respond?" *Parameters*, Autumn 2001, p. 117.

85. Jack Spencer, "The National Guard and Homeland Security," *Heritage Foundation Executive Memorandum No. 826*, July 29, 2002. www.heritage.org.

86. Jon Powers and Robert Stephenson, "On Guard in America: The National Guard Provides Homeland Defense," *USA Today*, March 2002, p. 11.

87. White House Office of Homeland Security, *National Strategy for Homeland Security*.

88. Ratnesar, "The State of Our Defense."

89. Quoted in Gorman and Freedberg, "A Burnt-Orange Nation," p. 638.

90. Quoted in Omestad, "Are We Safer?" p. 61.

91. White House Office of Homeland Security, *National Strategy for Homeland Security*.

92. Quoted in J. Michael Waller, "Security Blanket," *Insight on the News*, July 22, 2002, p. 12.

93. Quoted in Alex Fryer, "Feds Guide, Can't Enforce Tight Security at Local Level," *Seattle Times*, May 18, 2003, p. A1.

94. Fryer, "Feds Guide, Can't Enforce Tight Security at Local Level."

95. Quoted in Fryer, "Feds Guide, Can't Enforce Tight Security at Local Level."

96. Quoted in Sara Kershaw, "Terror Scenes Follow Script of Never Again," *New York Times*, May 13, 2003. www.nytimes. com.

Glossary

CDC: Centers for Disease Control and Prevention

CDP: Center for Domestic Preparedness

CERT: Community Emergency Response Teams

DHS: Department of Homeland Security

DOE: Department of Energy

DTRA: Defense Threat Reduction Agency

EMS: Emergency Medical Services

EMT: Emergency Medical Technician

ESDP: Executive Session on Domestic Preparedness

FEMA: Federal Emergency Management Agency

HHS: Department of Health and Human Services

HPAC: Hazard Prediction Assessment Capability

MMRS: Metropolitan Medical Response System

NDMS: National Disaster Medical System

NIPC: National Infrastructure Protection Center

NODP : National Office of Domestic Preparedness

NPS: National Pharmaceutical Stockpile

ODP: Office of Domestic Preparedness

OEM: Office of Emergency Management

RDD: Radiological Dispersion Device

SWAT: Special Weapons and Tactics

WMD: Weapons of Mass Destruction

For Further Reading

Book

Kathlyn Gay, *Silent Death: The Threat of Chemical and Biological Terrorism*. Brookfield, CT: Twenty-First Century Books, 2001. Geared toward middle schoolers, this text provides an overview of harmful biological and chemical agents and some incidents of their uses in history.

Internet Sources

Council on Foreign Relations (CFR) Task Force, "America–Still Unprepared, Still in Danger," CFR, 2002. www.cfr.org. This report highlights America's greatest vulnerabilities and recommends measures to address them.

Websites

Analytical Services Inc., ANSER Institute for Homeland Security (www.homelandsecurity.org). The institute is a nonprofit, nonpartisan think tank that works to educate the public about homeland security issues. The institute's website contains a virtual library of fact sheets, reports, legislation, and government documents and statistics on homeland security issues.

Department of Homeland Security (DHS) (www.dhs.gov). The creation of the DHS in March 2003 was the most significant transformation of the U.S. government since 1947. The DHS website offers a wide variety of information on homeland security, including press releases, speeches and testimonies, and reports on topics such as airport security, weapons of mass destruction, planning for and responding to emergencies, the DHS threat advisory system, and border control.

RAND (www.rand.org). RAND, an independent public policy think tank, offers a variety of online publications dealing with terrorist threats and homeland security policies.

READY.GOV (www.ready.gov). This website, sponsored by the DHS, is the federal government's principal online tool for providing information to the public about how to prepare for terrorist attacks.

Terrorism: Questions & Answers (www.terrorismanswers.com). This website, sponsored by the Council on Foreign Relations, provides information on a wide range of terrorism-related issues ranging from the various terrorist networks worldwide to the government's efforts to counter the threat of weapons of mass destruction.

Works Consulted

Book

National Research Council, *Making the Nation Safer: The Role of Science and Technology for Countering Terrorism.* Washington, DC: National Academies Press, 2002. Though the focus is on finding technological solutions to homeland security problems, this book provides a good overview of various terrorist threats and the measures being taken in response to them.

Periodicals

Graham Allison, "Encounter: Graham Allison," *Boston Globe*, December 1, 2002.

Graham Allison and Andrei Kokoshin, "The New Containment: An Alliance Against Nuclear Terrorism," *National Interest*, Fall 2002.

Guy F. Arnet, "What You Can Do to Protect Yourself Against Chemical, Biological, and Nuclear Terrorism," *Backwoods Home Magazine*, May/June 2003.

Randy Atkins, "The News Media Could Be Our Weakest Link," *Washington Post*, January 26, 2003.

Bioterrorism Week, "Terror Threat Extends to Common Chemicals, Officials Warn," April 28, 2003.

Kevin Coonan, "One Year Later: Emergency Department Response to Biological Terrorism Part II: Smallpox, Viral Hemorrhagic Fevers, Tularemia, and Botulinum Toxins," *Trauma Reports*, November/December 2002.

Dale Craig, "Communicating in a Crisis," *Journal of Counterterrorism and Homeland Security International*, Fall 2003.

Mary Dalrymple, "Federal, State or Local Responsibility for Homeland Defense?" *CQ Weekly*, February 1, 2003.

Ruth David, "Homeland Security: Building a National Strategy," *The Bridge*, Spring 2002.

Sarah Estabrooks, "Nuclear Terrorism," *Ploughshares Monitor*, December 2001.

Gorman Freedberg, "Beyond the Blue Canaries," *National Journal*, March 1, 2003.

Alex Fryer, "Feds Guide, Can't Enforce Tight Security at Local Level," *Seattle Times*, May 18, 2003.

Siobhan Gorman and Sydney J. Freedberg Jr., "A Burnt-Orange Nation," *National Journal*, March 1, 2003.

Spenser Hsu, "Worst-Case Scenario: Code Red Means It's Time to Put Plans into Action," *Washington Post*, March 16, 2003.

Human Events, "Forewarned, but Not Forestalled?" May 27, 2002.

Rebecca Katz, "Public Health Preparedness: The Best Defense Against Biological Weapons," *Provocations*, Summer 2002.

Alexandra Marks, "Flying the Fortified Skies," *Christian Science Monitor*, April 25, 2003.

Liz Marlantes and Abraham McLaughlin, "Gauging the Seriousness of New Terror Warnings," *Christian Science Monitor*, May 23, 2002.

Abraham McLaughlin and Michelle Dent, "Lesson for U.S. Cities from Antiterror Drills," *Christian Science Monitor*, May 15, 2003.

Michelle Mittlestadt, "Bioterror Focus May Obscure Greater Risk," *Dallas Morning News*, October 30, 2001.

Johanna Neuman, "Mass Evacuations Present Massive Problems," *Los Angeles Times*, May 11, 2003.

Bill Nichols, Mimi Hall, and Peter Eisner, "The Next Terror Threat—'The Future Is Here, I'm Afraid,'" *USA Today*, June 11, 2002.

Thomas Omestad, "Are We Safer?" *U.S. News & World Report*, September 2002.

Laura Parker et al., "Secure Often Means Secret," *USA Today*, May 16, 2002.

Douglas Pasternak, "A Nuclear Nightmare," *U.S. News & World Report*, September 17, 2001.

Bob Port, "Nuclear Terrorism: A 'Near-Term' Threat," *New York Daily News*, September 8, 2002.

Jon Powers and Robert Stephenson, "On Guard in America: The National Guard Provides Homeland Defense," *USA Today*, March 2002.

Johnna A. Pro, "Homeland Security Affecting Emphasis of Local Fire Stations," *Pittsburgh Post-Gazette*, May 25, 2003.

Chitra Ragavan et al., "Alert—and Anxious," *U.S. News & World Report*, March 31, 2001.

Romesh Ratnesar, "The State of Our Defense," *Time*, February 24, 2003.

Ron Scherer, "A Homeland Reader for 'High' Alert," *Christian Science Monitor*, March 20, 2003.

Rachel Smolkin, "Girding for Terror," *American Journalism Review*, April 2003.

John J. Stanton, "Is the U.S. Prepared for Nuclear Terrorism?" *Security Management*, March 2002.

Jonathan B. Tucker and Amy Sands, "An Unlikely Threat," *Bulletin of Atomic Scientists*, July 1999.

USA Today, "Color-Coded Terror Alerts Too Difficult to Decipher," September 26, 2002.

J. Michael Waller, "Security Blanket," *Insight on the News*, July 22, 2002.

Aaron Weiss, "When Terror Strikes, Who Should Respond?" *Parameters*, Autumn 2001.

Rick Weiss, "Anthrax Response Plans Inadequate, Study Warns," *Washington Post*, March 18, 2003.

Internet Sources

American Red Cross, "Terrorism: Preparing for the Unexpected." October 2001. www.redcross.org.

Joseph A. Barbera et al., "Ambulances to Nowhere: America's Critical Shortfall in Medical Preparedness for Catastrophic Terrorism,"

BCSIA Discussion Paper 2001-15, ESDP Discussion Paper ESDP-2001-07, John F. Kennedy School of Government, Harvard University, October 2001. www.homelanddefense.org.

George W. Bush, "State of the Union," White House, January 29, 2002. www.whitehouse.gov.

Centers for Disease Control and Prevention, "National Pharmaceutical Stockpile," *Public Health Emergency Preparedness and Response*. www.bt.cdc.gov.

Council on Foreign Relations, "Hospital Emergency Rooms," *Terrorism: Questions & Answers*. www.terrorismanswers.com.

Council on Foreign Relations, "Responding to Chemical Attacks," *Terrorism: Questions & Answers*. www.terrorismanswers.com.

Council on Foreign Relations, "Weapons of Mass Destruction: Anthrax," *Terrorism: Questions & Answers*. www.terrorism answers.com.

Council on Foreign Relations Task Force, "America–Still Unprepared, Still in Danger," Council on Foreign Relations, 2002. www.cfr.org.

Department of Homeland Security, "National Security Emergencies," *Emergencies and Disasters: Planning and Prevention*. www.dhs.gov.

Department of Homeland Security, "Smallpox Frequently Asked Questions," *Threats & Protection*. www.dhs.gov.

David Eberhart, "Fallout Shelters Fall Short in the U.S.," *NewsMax.com*, February 15, 2002. www.newsmax.com.

Emergency Survival Program, "Learn Light Search and Rescue," ESP FOCUS, August 2003. www.cert-la.com.

Executive Session on Domestic Preparedness, "A New National Priority: Enhancing Public Health and Safety Through Domestic Preparedness," *Perspectives on Preparedness*, March 2001. http://bcsia.ksg.harvard.edu.

Executive Session on Domestic Preparedness, *Beyond the Beltway: Focusing on Hometown Security*, John F. Kennedy School of Government, Harvard University, September 2002. http://bcsia.ksg.harvard.edu.

Federal Emergency Management Agency, "FEMA Task Force Tools

and Equipment," *Urban Search and Rescue Response System*. www.fema.gov.

Federal Emergency Management Agency, *Managing the Emergency Consequences of Terrorist Incidents: Interim Planning Guide for State and Local Governments*, July 2002. www.fema.org.

FEMA News, "Homeland Security Helps Train Citizens for Emergencies with $19 Million for Community Emergency Response Teams," May 29, 2003. www.fema.gov.

Brian Michael Jenkins, *Terrorism: Current and Long Term Threats*, testimony before the Senate Armed Services Subcommittee on Emerging Threats, November 15, 2001. www.rand.org.

Johns Hopkins Center for Civilian Biodefense, "Viral Hemorrhagic Fevers Fact Sheet." www.hopkins-biodefense.org.

Henry Kelly, *Testimony on Terrorist Nuclear Threat*, testimony before the Senate Committee on Foreign Relations, March 6, 2002. www.fas.org.

Sara Kershaw, "Terror Scenes Follow Script of Never Again," *New York Times*, May 13, 2003. www.nytimes.com.

Beverly Lumpkin, "Terror Test," *abcNEWS.com*, May 12, 2003. http://more.abcnews.go.com.

Viktor Mayer-Schönberger, "Emergency Communications: The Quest for Interoperability in the United States and Europe," BCSIA Discussion Paper 2002-7, ESDP Discussion Paper ESDP-2002-03, John F. Kennedy School of Government, Harvard University, March 2002. http://ksgnotes1.harvard.edu.

Jack Spencer, "The National Guard and Homeland Security," *Heritage Foundation Executive Memorandum No. 826*, July 29, 2002. www.heritage.org.

UF News, "University of Florida Surgeon Calls on Medical Personnel to Revamp Terrorist Plans," September 6, 2002. www.napa.ufl.edu.

White House Office of Homeland Security, *National Strategy for Homeland Security*, July 2002. www.whitehouse.gov.

Index

Picture Credits

About the Author

James D. Torr is a freelance writer and editor who has worked on a variety of publications for Greenhaven Press and Lucent Books.